CIVIL AUTHORITY IN MEDIEVAL PHILOSOPHY

Lombard, Aquinas and Bonaventure

Michael P. Malloy

UNIVERSITY
PRESS OF
AMERICA

LANHAM • NEW YORK • LONDON

Copyright © 1985 by Michael P. Malloy

University Press of America,™ Inc.

4720 Boston Way
Lanham, MD 20706

3 Henrietta Street
London WC2E 8LU England

All rights reserved
Printed in the United States of America

Library of Congress Cataloging in Publication Data

Malloy, Michael P., 1951-
  Civil authority in Medieval philosophy.

  Revision of thesis (doctoral)—Georgetown University, Washington, D.C.
  Includes bibliographical references and index.
  1. Philosophy, Medieval. 2. Authority. 3. Sin. 4. Obedience. 5. Thomas, Aquinas, Saint, 1225?-1274. 6. Bonaventure, Saint, Cardinal, ca. 1217-1274. 7. Peter Lombard, Bishop of Paris, ca. 1100-1160. I. Title.
  B738.A87M35   1985   172'.1   85-3210
  ISBN 0-8191-4582-3 (alk. paper)
  ISBN 0-8191-4583-1 (pbk. : alk. paper)

All University Press of America books are produced on acid-free paper which exceeds the minimum standards set by the National Historical Publications and Records Commission.

In memoriam,

Francis Edward Malloy
1925-1983

ACKNOWLEDGEMENTS

The author wishes to express his sincere gratitude to Dr. Thomas P. McTighe, of Georgetown University, who served as mentor for an earlier version of this work in the form of a doctoral dissertation. His guidance was gifted and essential. Thanks must also be extended to Dr. Wilfrid Desan, Professor Emeritus of Georgetown University, whose valued friendship and advice are both much appreciated. In addition, as a practical matter much of the early work leading to the preparation of the present study would have been nearly impossible but for the kind hospitality and forbearance of my good friends, Dr. and Mrs. Louis N. Pangaro.

Finally, the author must thank his wife for her patience and moral support throughout the many trials and tribulations leading to the completion of this work.

The Latin works in English translation throughout this book were prepared by the author. As to references to the works of Aristotle, the reader's attention is directed to the excellent Random House edition of the Basic Works of Aristotle, edited by Richard McKeon. I gratefully acknowledge the permission of the copyright holder to quote from the following work:

Chenu, Toward Understanding Saint Thomas. Trans. by A.-M. Landry & D. Hughes. Chicago: Henry Regnery Co., 1964. Used by permission of Regnery Gateway, Inc.

TABLE OF CONTENTS

FOREWORD xi

TRANSLATOR'S INTRODUCTION: AN ESSAY
IN COMPARATIVE ANALYSIS 1

   I. The Context of the Problem 3

  II. The Problem of Civil Authority
      in Lombard's *Sentences* 24

 III. Aquinas' Sentential Commentary . . 45

  IV. Aquinas' Later Writings 83

   V. Bonaventure's Sentential
      Commentary 104

PART I: SELECTION FROM THE *SENTENCES*
       OF PETER LOMBARD 135

On the Potential for Sin: Whether it
   exists in Man or the Devil from God . . 137

Authorities affirm the Notion that
   the Potential for Sin is from God . . . 138

Whether there may ever be Resistance
   to Authority 139

PART II: EXCERPTS FROM THE COMMENTARY
        OF THOMAS AQUINAS 141

Textual Analysis 143

First Question 144

    First Article: Whether the poten-
      tial for sin comes from God . . . 145

    Second Article: Whether all
      sovereignty comes from God 149

    Third Article: Whether in
      the state of innocence

there was a civil power 152

Second Question 155

    First Article: Whether
        obedience is a virtue 156

    Second Article: Whether Christians
        are required to obey secular
        authorities, and especially
        absolute rulers 161

    Third Article: Whether the religious are required to obey their
        prelates in all things 165

Literal Exposition 169

PART III: EXCERPTS FROM THE COMMENTARY
         OF BONAVENTURE 175

Textual Analysis 177

Treatment of the Questions 178

Article I: In what does the power
  for sin have its origin 179

    Question I: Whether the potential
        for sin arises in us from God . . 179

    Question II: Whether the potential for sin, understood in
        that way, is evil 184

Article II: Concerning the power
  for governing 189

    Question I: Whether every power
        for ruling comes from God 190

    Question II: Whether the power
        for governing is in man as a
        natural institution or as a
        punishment for guilt 195

Article III: Concerning the necessity for
  subjection to the governing power . . . 200

Question I: Whether Christians are required to be subject to rulers or a secular power in some things 201

Question II: Whether the religious are required to obey their prelates in all things which are not contrary to God 207

Doubts concerning the Writings of the Master 211

INDEX 217

FOREWORD

This book is intended to fulfill a two-fold purpose. In terms of its substantive inquiry, it concerns a critical examination of the concept of civil authority as expressed in certain selected writings of Thomas Aquinas and Bonaventure.[1] Thus, it is concerned with answers to the following questions: (i) What is the source of civil authority? (ii) How far must one obey those invested with civil authority?

However, in terms of its methodological inquiry, this book is concerned with the following issues: (i) Does the existence of a sentential commentary[2] for almost every medieval thinker who aspired to the title of *magister*, replying to precisely the same question posed in precisely the same way, offer a productive tool for comparative analysis of the positions of these thinkers? (ii) More specifically, does an analysis of Aquinas' sentential commentary provide a useful source of data to examine the development of his thought?

The underlying thesis of this analysis is that the two methodological questions can be answered in the affirmative. It may therefore be surprising that the methodology followed in this book has been relatively neglected to date.[3]

Abstractly, it would seem that Aquinas' sentential commentary, representing his first

---

[1] Specifically, this examination shall be limited to Aquinas' and Bonaventure's commentaries on the *Sentences* of Peter Lombard (hereinafter "sentential commentaries"), and other later writings of Aquinas.

[2] I.e., any commentary on the *Sentences* of Peter Lombard. (See note 1 supra.) For much of the medieval period, the sentential commentary was a requirement for the title of *magister*.

[3] The sentential commentary itself is not available in extended English translation. Small portions of two questions from Distinction 44, the subject of the present study, do appear in translation in Thomas Aquinas, *Selected Political*

extended and organized examination of a range of philosophical and theological problems, should hold a place of some significance in the study of his corpus. The sentential commentary is the place at which Aquinas may have made some of his basic choices as a thinker. Chenu tells us that Aquinas

> began his personal efforts and made his choices in doctrine and methodology through a commentary upon the IV Libri Sententiarum. Indeed, the two years that he had previously been obliged to devote "cursory reading" of the Bible, however meaningful they may have been as regards the medieval regime of theological knowledge, could play only a limited role in the determining of his choices. Thus, after the years 1252-1254 during which he had just fulfilled the tasks of the baccalaureus biblicus (Bachelor of the Bible), Brother Thomas was to comment on Peter Lombard. . . .[4]

Thus, it is in his sentential commentary that we may encounter Aquinas in his first effort at independent reflection. It must be stressed, however, that the importance of the sentential commentary asserted by Chenu is not simply an instance of pride of place; there is more at stake than the incidental historical fact that this commentary was Aquinas' first independent effort. To the contrary, Chenu emphasizes that the sentential commentary was the place where Aquinas "established his basic positions,"[5] and it was there "his master intuitions already held sway."[6]

Writings, ed. A.P. d'Entreves, Trans. J.G. Dawson (Oxford: Basil Blackwell, 1948), pp. 181-87.

[4]M.-D. Chenu, Toward Understanding Saint Thomas, trans. A.-M. Landry, O.P. and D. Hughes, O.P. (Chicago: Henry Regnery Company, 1964), p. 264 (footnote omitted).

[5]Chenu, p. 272.

[6]Ibid.

Accordingly, then, Chenu asserts the importance of Aquinas' sentential commentary on the basis of its merits as an instance of philosophical reflection.

This opinion receives the concurrence of at least one scholar who has devoted an extended work to Aquinas' sentential commentary itself. Mondin has enthusiastically asserted the primacy of the commentary, both in terms of its chronology and in terms of its substance:

> The Commentary to the Sentences... ranks first in the long list of Aquinas' works, not only in the orders of time and space (in extension it surpasses even the big Summa Theologiae) but also as to its speculative vigor, originality and profoundness of thought. In this work one finds all of the most characteristic elements of his philosophy.[7]

This assertion of centrality for the commentary is certainly an extremely bold one, and it must be critically evaluated. Indeed, one of Mondin's basic theses in his study is that "the Scripta is St. Thomas' most impressive, monumental in order to justify a study devoted to the sentential commentary and fundamental work, and therefore deserves a study of its own...."[8] It may well be that this position borders on the foolhardy. Certainly, at the very least it asserts more than it need assert in order to justify a study devoted to the sentential commentary.

It may be, however, that Mondin may be excused his enthusiasm when one considers the paucity of scholarly literature which is in fact devoted to Aquinas' sentential commentary. Aside from Mondin's

---

[7]Battista Mondin, St. Thomas Aquinas' Philosophy in the Commentary to the Sentences (The Hague: Martinus Nijhoff, 1975), p. 1. Indeed, in support of the above quotation, Mondin cites Chenu in a footnote.

[8]Ibid., p. 2

study,[9] as well as a few other works like Stevaux's study of the doctrine of charity in Aquinas' sentential commentary and certain of his contemporaries,[10] there has been relatively little in the way of study devoted primarily to the sentential commentary of Aquinas.

The contributions of the sentential commentary to the topic of civil authority have been largely neglected if not completely ignored. At the very least, however, influential commentators such as the Carlyles have recognized the significance of the turn in Aquinas from "Augustinian" notions of convention to the "Aristotelian" theme of the socio-political nature of man.[11] The view that the turn from the "conventional" to the "natural" character of political institutions is a significant development in the history of political theory is shared by such diverse commentators as Morrall,[12] Ullmann,[13] and d'Entreves.[14]

Hence, in the introductory essay which follows, and more particularly in the primary texts, we shall

---

[9] In fact, Mondin's study itself does not deal with issues of political philosophy, like the problem of civil authority, which appear in the commentary.

[10] See A. Stevaux, "La doctrine de la charite dans les commentaires des Sentences de S. Albert, S. Bonaventure, S. Thomas," Ephemerides Theologicae Lovanienes 24 (1948):59-97, cited in Chenu, p. 278.

[11] See R.W. & A.J. Carlyle, A History of Medieval Political Theory in the West, vol. 3: Political Theory from the Tenth Century to the Thirteenth (London: W. Blackwood and Sons, 1928), p. 3.

[12] See J.B. Morrall, Political Thought in Medieval Times (New York: Harper Torchbooks, 1962), p. 69.

[13] See Walter Ullmann, A History of Political Thought: The Middle Ages (Baltimore: Penguin Books, 1968), p. 175.

[14] See A.P. d'Entreves, The Medieval Contribution to Political Thought (Oxford: Oxford University Press 1939), pp. 22-3.

have an opportunity to examine a conceptual
transformation in political theory which may
constitute one of the most characteristic features of
medieval political philosophy.[15]

                         Michael P. Malloy, J.D., Ph.D.
                         Associate Professor of Law

Seton Hall University
Newark, New Jersey

October 1984

---

[15] Cf. *ibid.*, p. 35.

TRANSLATOR'S INTRODUCTION:
AN ESSAY IN COMPARATIVE ANALYSIS

TRANSLATOR'S INTRODUCTION:
AN ESSAY IN COMPARATIVE ANALYSIS

I. THE CONTEXT OF THE PROBLEM

The Academic Environment

Though one need not go as far as d'Entreves does in emphasizing the relative seclusion of Aquinas' life as a scholar and religious,[1] still it cannot be denied that the academic environment was of notable importance to the development of Aquinas' thought. This environment has obvious significance for purposes of the present analysis, since the dual comparative method to be employed here hopes to capitalize on a specific aspect of that environment, the institutionalized method of commentary.

As Morrall has noted,[2] one of the basic activities of university education during the medieval period of Aquinas was the preparation of commentaries on noted authorities (auctoritates). These authorities apparently came to include not only primary (typically, patristic) texts, but also collocations of pertinent passages of such texts. This type of compendium, in the nature of a textbook had been attempted by Abelard in philosophy, and later by Peter Lombard in theology. Lombard's collection of patristic opinions (sententiae) included modest commentary by Lombard himself, weaving together the passages into a unified and organized textbook.

---

[1] A.P. d'Entreves, Introduction to Selected Political Writings, by Thomas Aquinas (Oxford: Basil Blackwell, 1948), p. vii.

[2] See John B. Morrall, Political Thought in Medieval Times (New York: Harper Torchbooks, 1962), p. 49.

Of particular interest, of course, is the fact that Lombard's Sentences was gradually to become one of the basic texts for commentary at the University of Paris and elsewhere for those aspiring to the magister. Its insinuation into the curriculum was, if not swift, at least apparently inexorable. Lombard, a Twelfth Century theologian,[3] completed the Sentences around 1152.[4] Throughout the last third of the Twelfth Century, the text was used by various masters as a textbook, particularly by Lombard's follower Peter of Poitiers at the school of Notre Dame de Paris.[5] Its primacy as an official textbook was no doubt assured by the approval it received from the Lateran Council in 1215.[6]

Following that approval, it soon became the general practice in the Faculty of Theology to do a public "reading"[7] of the Sentences as a prerequisite

---

[3]There is some uncertainty about the precise dates of Lombard's life. Father Brady gives 1095-1160. (The Encyclopedia of Philosophy, 1972 Reprint ed., s.v. "Peter Lombard," by Ignatius Brady.) Professor Henry prefers 1100-1160. (Ibid., s.v. "Medieval Philosophy," by Desmond Paul Henry.) Morrall agrees as to the date of death. (Morrall, p. 49.) In any event, therefore, the Sentences comes towards the end of Lombard's career.

[4]See M.-D. Chenu, Toward Understanding Saint Thomas, trans. A.-M. Landry and D. Hughes (Chicago: Henry Regnery Company, 1964), p. 265.

[5]See, e.g., ibid.: "From the last third of the XIIth century, certain masters . . . were already using it as a textbook, and the plan of its treatises, even when their speculative or practical lacunae were recognized, was rather generally adopted."

[6]Ibid.

[7]I.e., the lectio, a formal series of lectures

for the <u>magister</u> in theology. By 1222 Alexander of Hales, Bonaventure's mentor, was utilizing the <u>Sentences</u> as a basic text in his course.[8] Chenu identifies the period around 1230 as the next stage along the way of the primacy of the <u>Sentences</u>:

> Around 1230, one might say, the <u>Book of Sentences</u> had become the official text at the moment when the teaching of theology was split into two stages, with the master, titular of a chair, "reading" Scripture, while his young collaborator, the bachelor, took the four books of the <u>Sentences</u> as his text, whence his title, <u>baccalaureus</u> <u>sententiarius</u>. . . . In 1254, this arrangement was the basis of all University regulations.[9]

Thus, this text became an institutionalized part of the academic experience of Aquinas and his contemporaries at Paris and elsewhere.[10] Hence, we confront a situation in which this one text is a touchstone in the early careers of virtually all of those who participated in the flowering of medieval theology and philosophy, at least those who pursued their studies in a faculty of theology rather than arts. By the time Aquinas undertook his <u>lectio</u> on this text from 1254 to 1256,[11] the <u>Sentences</u> was the <u>textus</u> for the magistral aspirant at the University of Paris. Its influence continued to spread: "From this starting point [at the University of Paris], it gradually extended over a period of three centuries to all universities of Christendom."[12]

Lombard's <u>Sentences</u> had in fact preempted the academic institutional context which Aquinas

---

on a set text. See <u>ibid</u>., pp. 80-85.

[8]See Brady, "Peter Lombard," supra note 3.

[9]Chenu, p. 265.

[10]Brady, supra note 3.

[11]Chenu, p. 82.

[12]<u>Ibid</u>., p. 265.

confronted as he began his intellectual career.[13] For a thinker who was to lead, and indeed to a great extent initiate, the project of assimilation of Aristotelianism into Christian theology and philosophy, this circumstance must appear curious, for Lombard's orientation was essentially Augustinian. To the extent that this formula of Augustinianism comprised a part of the institutional requirements facing Aquinas as a sentential commentator, therefore, the challenge to his project of assimilation would confront him squarely almost at the outset of his academic career. Indeed, the confrontation was unavoidable since, as Chenu has emphasized, Lombard's Sentences

> was a modest but clever compilation of Augustinian thoughts and texts. . . . The Book of Sentences became the manual universally used and the basic matter being taught in the universities. The unheard of success it enjoyed at the Lateran council of 1215 served to determine once and for all the school tradition that would exist within the framework of Western theology and would bar any rival attempts seeking to reinforce their positions with help from the Greek doctors.[14]

Hence, Aquinas did not simply confront in his project the opposition of a general nature among his teachers and colleagues, not the informal bias of an attitude or a "spirit" within the University. He found that the contrasting attitude of Augustinianism was a formal part of the structure of his academic environment. On the other hand, he could, and apparently did, rely upon the fact that the lectio of the baccalaureus sententiarius already in his time had progressed beyond a mere literal

---

[13]See generally Edward A. Synan, "Brother Thomas, the Master and the Masters," in St. Thomas Aquinas: 1274-1974 Commemorative Studies, 2 vols. (Toronto: Pontifical Institute of Medieval Studies, 1974), 2:232-40.

[14]Chenu, p. 52.

exposition of the text.[15] In the sentential commentary, therefore, the fledgling process of assimilation could advance, but only within the preordained framework afforded by the Augustinian text. Still, since the sentential <u>lectio</u> had already gone beyond a mere exposition, there was considerable margin for Aquinas to set forth an elaboration of philosophical problems which expressed something approximating his own independent thought. This margin was itself part of the institutional setting in which Aquinas found himself as a <u>baccalaureus sententiarius</u>. In this regard Chenu has noted:

> The <u>Sentences</u> of the Lombard were themselves subjected to . . . immoderate handling. In a half-century, they passed from a regime of glossing to one of questions increasingly posited, treated, and organized outside the original text. . . .
> We have reached, therefore, a point beyond the Lombard. The <u>Hic quaeritur</u> by which the Lombard himself had introduced the questions in his <u>Sentences</u> had been the starting-point, it is true, of . . . speculative elaboration. Their number multiplied to such a degree, however, brings us, theologically speaking, to another literary and doctrinal genre.[16]

Nevertheless, it would seem to be almost essential for Aquinas later on to decide "to build a <u>summa</u> freed from the framework and constraints

---

[15]Ibid., p. 267: Lombard's <u>Sentences</u> "was permeated with Augustinian vigor and organized into the categories of Augustine--of an Augustine whose stimulating metaphysical purviews and religious experiences would at any rate have to be toned down for the use of good students. . . . [W]hen Saint Thomas arrived on the scene, the teaching of the <u>Sentences</u> . . . had already gone far beyond the <u>expositio</u> of the text."

[16]Ibid., p. 270.

imposed by the Sentences. . . ."[17] Notwithstanding the necessity of this further development, and the pride of place since given to the Summa by students of Aquinas' philosophy, we should acknowledge the achievement of his sentential commentary. This commentary having been redacted immediately upon its completion in 1256, we find that

> at the age of 30, Saint Thomas had already presented to his contemporaries a general expose of his entire thought on all theological subjects under discussion.[18]

While his sentential commentary affords us a useful and direct point of contact with the work of his contemporaries, Aquinas' Summa was to eclipse not only that commentary, but eventually even the textus which was its nominal subject. Cajetan,[19] perhaps best known for his commentary on the Summa Theologiae, is thought to be the first to replace the Sentences with the Summa as an official theological textbook.[20] Thus we may mark this change as heralding the end of the long period of influence of the Sentences. In fact, it may be argued, that period was ending by virtue of the very act of the production of the Summa itself some two centuries before.

It is perhaps understandable that, given the subject of the present analysis, the place of the Sentences within the academic environment has been emphasized so far. We should not, however, ignore the fact that in Aquinas' time one of the most extraordinary features was without doubt the rediscovery (and eventual assimilation) of

---

[17]Ibid., p. 266.

[18]Ibid., p. 268.

[19]Cardinal Thomas de Vio (1469-1534).

[20]See Etienne Gilson, gen. ed., A History of Philosophy, 4 vols. (New York: Random House, 1962), vol. 2: Medieval Philosophy, by Armand A. Maurer, pp. 349-50.

Aristotelian philosophy by Medieval Europe.[21] The track of Aquinas' development through his writings is as much the history of the replacement of the "pure abstraction"[22] of Augustinianism with Aristotelian principles, in political theory as elsewhere. Indeed, Augustine's stress upon the power of sin over fallen man, and the implications of this emphasis for one's view of the legitimacy of the political community, will be at the heart of the "problem" of civil authority.

Still, it should be noted that Aquinas' project of assimilation of Aristotelianism did not entail a heavy-handed or absolute repudiation of the Neoplatonic approach of Augustinianism. As we shall see in our examination of Aquinas' sentential commentary, Augustine remained an authority to be consulted. The project of assimilation is more complex than a simple and exclusive synthesis between Christianity and Aristotle's philosophy. The academic environment within which Aquinas operated required a more subtle process of accommodation, and it provided the material for it.

Morrall seizes upon this important qualification in understanding the novel developments which Aquinas' philosophy impressed upon the Medieval philosophic community.[23] It is a distorted and inadequate view of Aquinas' impact upon that community to view his contribution as merely the synthesis of Faith and the Philosopher. The vibrant and, until then, premiere tradition of Augustinian Neoplatonism was called upon as well in the development of Aquinas' thought.

---

[21] For the Christian world, Paris was without doubt the center of this development. See, e.g., Jean Dunbabin, "Aristotle in the Schools," in Trends in Medieval Political Thought, ed. Beryl Smalley (Oxford: Basil Blackwell, 1965), pp. 66 et seq.

[22] Walter Ullmann, A History of Political Thought The Middle Ages. (Baltimore: Penguin Books, 1968), p. 173.

[23] See Morrall, p. 70.

Nevertheless, so long as this qualification is kept in mind, it is not distorted or simplistic to emphasize the obvious centrality of the project of assimilation in Aquinas' work. The success of this project is due to the availability of the newly discovered texts of the Aristotelian corpus.[24] The work of "purifying" (or, in less felicitous terms, to Christianize) the rediscovered philosophical works of Aristotle in the Thirteenth Century[25] fell principally to Albert, Aquinas' mentor, to Aquinas himself, and to William of Moerbeke, Aquinas' friend and colleague,[26] who provided translations of the Aristotelian texts into Latin.[27] Hence, the project of assimilation was not simply a dispassionate play of ideas. Quite to the contrary, it was an academic voyage of discovery.[28] While it is perhaps

---

[24]See generally Ullmann, pp. 159 et seq.; Chenu, pp. 31 et seq.

[25]The logical works had been generally known since the Eleventh Century. See Chenu, p. 32.

[26]They met at the court of Pope Urban IV in the 1260's. See The Encyclopedia of Philosophy, 1972 Reprint ed., s.v. "William of Moerbeke," by Eugene P. Fairweather.

[27]Ullmann, p. 171.

[28]With respect to this project, one writer has given the following somewhat fanciful (and apparently undocumented) description: "Aquinas, unlike Albert the Great, was not satisfied with and would not accept the current translations of the Stagyrite. At the saint's request permission was accorded two friars of his order, William of Moerbecke and Henry of Brabant, both accomplished Greek students, to

natural to assume that Aquine utilized the fruits of Moerbeke's labors as translator, the precise extent of the former's debt in this regard is not known. Moerbeke's translations were not the first available in the Thirteenth Century,[29] and Aquinas' sentential commentary, containing allusions to the Philosopher's thought, was completed at least four years before the two first met.

Concerning the academic environment in which Aquinas' sentential commentary was produced, then, we should note two features. First, Aquinas was working within a format which was already a traditional one, requiring a treatment of questions cast in an Augustinian mode and entailing the rendering of his own thought in a literal context which has immediate points of comparison with those who preceeded and followed him in the history of Medieval philosophy. Second, the academic environment was alive with the shock and challenge of the rediscovered Aristotelian corpus, which, as assimilated by Aquinas in the course of his academic career, would eventually eclipse the tradition manifested by the Sentences.

The Social and Political Milieu

In reflecting upon any aspect of a political philosophy, one might expect that the social and political milieu in which the philosophy was produced would be of some interest.[30] Both Aquinas

---

journey in search of original sources in order to compile a new translation of the works of the Stagyrite, and it was such transcriptions that provided the Angelic Doctor with a true version of Aristotle." D.T. Mullane, "Aristotelianism in St. Thomas" (Ph.D. dissertation, The Catholic University of America, 1929), p. 52. The reliance of Aquinas on these translations has been questioned. Fairweather, supra note 26.

[29]Fairweather, supra note 26.

[30]For a useful, general review of the social and political milieu of Aquinas' time, see Chenu, pp. 11-78. As to Bonaventure, an exact contemporary of Aquinas, see E. Gilson, The Philosophy of St.

and Bonaventure led lives of quiet scholarship and religious dedication.[31] While both in their time knew heated controversy,[32] some commentators have emphasized their detachment from the political milieu. In particular, d'Entreves is at pains to insist that particular details of Aquinas' life or of the period in which he lived not be read into any interpretation of his work, and particularly into those aspects of his work which may be considered his "political philosophy." Indeed, he was not, in any modern sense, a political thinker; those aspects of political theory which may find a place in his thought are properly placed in the broader context of his theological and metaphysical concerns.

At the other extreme from d'Entreves, however, are those commentators who would stress what they assert to be Aquinas' direct involvement in the political and social milieu of his time. Mullane has argued, for example:

> As a moralist Aquinas was always being consulted by persons of all degrees. . . . The Angelic Doctor can

---

Bonaventure, trans. I. Trethowan and F.J. Sheed (New York: Sheed & Ward, 1940), pp. 1-86.

[31] For summaries of Aquinas' life, see F. Copleston, A History of Philosophy: vol. 2: Medieval Philosophy (Garden City, N.Y.: Image Books, 1962), pp. 20-22; Chenu, pp. 11-14. For a summary of Bonaventure's life, see Gilson, pp. 1 et seq.

[32] It is an interesting coincidence that, as a result of one of the many controversies between the University and the Mendicant Orders, it required a Papal Bull on October 2, 1257, before the University would receive Aquinas and Bonaventure as doctors. See Gilson, pp. 10-14.

[33] A.P. d'Entreves, p. vii.

> also be considered as an initiator initiator and organizer of thought.
>
> ... He was in constant demand to give courses at Paris, Cologne, Rome, Naples, and at the various Papal courts at Viterbo, Orvieto, and Renigiae. ...
>
> Owing to Thomas' varied talents he was in constant demand and travelled extensively, being entrusted with diplomatic missions. For instance he was the esteemed confidant of Pope Urban IV. In 1256 he appeared before Pope Alexander IV, representing the religious orders against which antagonism had arisen in the University of Paris. Likewise in his own religious community he filled many important executive offices. ...[34]

In the present writer's view, the image of the man of affairs implied by the above argument seems strained. Aquinas should not be mistaken for a roving statesman. The achievements of his career are to be found in his writings. Undoubtedly, it may have been against just such attractive yet ultimately unbalanced views that d'Entreves was directing his remarks concerning the superfluity of biographical details, almost as a corrective. Yet surely the most accurate view must lie somewhere between these extremes. Gilson's remarks concerning Bonaventure's career may, to some degree, be applicable to Aquinas as well, though the latter was never head of his order:

> Obviously such a life is not that of a pure philosopher. It was not given over totally to the contemplation of abstract truths. St. Bonaventure is not only the leader of a philosophical school, an extremely fertile writer, a theologian and a mystic; he is likewise a man of action: this

---

[34]Mullane, pp. 70-71.

>administrator of a great religious Order is of the race of leaders of men.[35]

To be sure, even d'Entreves himself is willing to grant at least some degree of political awareness to Aquinas.[36] He does not deny that Aquinas must have been at least acquainted with his contemporary political situation, nor need he deny this for his previous comments to have force. The point is not that Aquinas was naive or insensible concerning the political milieu in which he lived. Rather, d'Entreves is arguing against speculation that would transform the indirect, essentially theoretical political aspects of Aquinas' thought into the product of reflection upon a practical involvement in that milieu.

We shall have occasion to see later that Aquinas' views may stem more from principles of philosophical anthropology than practical experience. Of course, the adoption by Aquinas of an Aristotelian notion of man as by nature political and social, as opposed to the notion of fallen man who needs to repudiate the earthly city in favor of the heavenly one, is in accord with the stirrings of nationalism to be seen in the later Medieval period.[37] The events of his times may be seen as providing a particularly hospitable environment for the growth of a political philosophy which affords man a positive place within society and political institutions. Morrall has noted this fact,[38] and points out that the Thirteenth Century was an age in which political centralization, whether by king or pope, was beginning to make itself felt. To the extent that

---

[35]Gilson, p. 35.

[36]See, e.g., A.P. d'Entreves, pp. vii-viii.

[37]See, e.g., *ibid*., p. x.

[38]See Morrall, pp. 68-69.

this emerging centralization manifested itself in the lives of the people, it would naturally be more difficult to assume uncritically that man had no positive place in this natural milieu. It was fortuitous indeed that, in an age in which the conditions for a more positive, active role for the civil community was becoming apparent, Aristotle was to make his reappearance. Within the Aristotelian perspective, man was essentially a political animal; hence, civil authority ought to be viewed as in some sense natural, not the punishment imposed for the fallen nature of man.

Aquinas' age was one of profound social and political change,[39] particularly in terms of the orientation of the individual towards political institutions. Aside from the continuing and tedious struggle between pope and emperor for supremacy,[40] the age presented the conditions for a fundamental reevaluation of the traditional, Augustinian notion that political institutions existed as mere conventions imposed for the punishment of the wicked and the testing of the faithful. Aristotelian

---

[39] See, e.g., E. Gilson, Dante the Philosopher, trans. David Moore (New York: Sheed & Ward, 1949).

[40] For the background of this struggle, see R.W. & A.J. Carlyle, A History of Mediaeval Political Theory in the West, vol. III: Political Theory from the Tenth Century to the Thirteenth (London: W. Blackwood & Sons, 1928), p. 16 et seq.; ibid., vol. IV: The Theories of the Relation of the Empire and the Papacy from the Tenth Century to the Twelfth, pp. 2, 42 et seq.

thought suggested that political institutions were natural to man, and this suggested realignment of man's relation to society raised serious problems for any coherent philosophy. It is the need to solve that problem which provides the specific background of Aquinas' commentary.

The "Problem" of Civil Authority

The immediate intellectual context of Aquinas' commentary is a traditional "problem" of civil authority. This problem can be characterized in several distinct, though related, ways.

First, in the sense most immediate to the milieu in which Aquinas found himself, the problem of civil authority is represented by the question of whether to accept the displacement of the conventional view of authority with the natural view. Of course, the conventional view had its affinity for the position that the pope held primacy over the temporal lord, a view endorsed by such thinkers as John of Salisbury, relying on St. Paul and Isidore, who saw the temporal power as a tool for the punishment of the wicked.[41]

The clash between the traditional, Patristic view of political authority and the rediscovered Aristotelian view has been well described by the Carlyles.[42] Essentially, each side in the controversy drew inspiration from alternative views of the nature of man. If man is essentially a free being -- radically free, constrained only by the revelation of God -- then manifestations of civil authority must be viewed as coercive. Such coercive authority has no inherent legitimacy and can only be rationalized as a necessary result of the fall of man's nature in the primordial transgression of divine constraints. On the other hand, if man is essentially a social or political being, not

---

[41]See, e.g., Ullmann, pp. 122-3.

[42]See R.W. & A.J. Carlyle, vol. III, p. 5.

radically free by nature, then it is open for one to argue that civil authority and other political institutions serve a natural function and an inherent value. In effect, the rediscovered Aristotelian texts afforded an authoritative basis for this latter argument.

In the earlier, traditional view, of course, the source of civil authority (and its limits) were thought to be clear. The authority comes from God and is judged simply by the degree to which it serves God's purposes:

> This is the real meaning of the doctrine of the New Testament, and the Fathers, and of the Middle Ages, that the authority of the king is a divine authority. He is God's minister for the punishment of the wicked and the reward of the good.[43]

Hence, the rediscovery of the Aristotelian view, based upon a philosophical anthropology (man's nature as political), rather than upon a theodicy, must have created a crisis for the Medieval view of the relation between church and the civil community, between *sacerdos* and *rex*. As Morrall notes,

> One can imagine the excitement and (in some cases) alarm with which the thinkers of the thirteenth century must have discovered this revolutionary theory. If Aristotle was to be taken at his word, the old conception of a unified Christian religious-political commonwealth must inevitably be modified to make room for a clear field of autonomy for the secular community.[44]

---

[43]*Ibid.*, pp. 182-3.

[44]Morrall, p. 69.

Of course, to some extent the Medieval intellect resisted the implications of this theory. At least in its formal terms, political theory failed to absorb completely the reorientation suggested by the rediscovery of Aristotelian principles. In a sense, Aquinas' political philosophy, such as it was, was more "modern" than anything to be seen until Rousseau, for Aquinas was willing to consider the possibility that political society and political obligation were something that arose out of the nature of man.[45]

Whether or not Aquinas would be willing to go so far, Morrall sees the natural view of civil authority as establishing a precondition for the autonomy of the political community:

> The concept of political society is thus detached from its previous connection in Christian thought with original sin, its consequences and remedies, and hence from any inherent connection with the economy of redemption and the Church, the channel through which the benefits are conveyed.[46]

Of course, for Aquinas even nature has its source in the divine, so that the crisis may not be quite so clearcut. Nevertheless, the precondition for political autonomy exists. Ullman emphasizes this implication of the natural view of civil authority:

> Thomas held that it was man's 'natural instinct' which brought

---

[45]See, e.g., Carlyle, vol. III, p. 5-6: "The formal conceptions of the Middle Ages were, however, on this point little affected by St. Thomas. It is evident that the conception of the conventional and 'unnatural' character of the state was too firmly fixed to be shaken even by his authority, and that it passed with little alteration . . . until Rousseau in the 'Contract Social' recovered the organic conception of the state. . . ."

[46]Morrall, p. 72.

> forth the State, that is, organized human society. Consequently, to Thomas, the State was a product of nature and therefore followed the laws of nature. It was 'natural reason which urges' this human association, and for the working of the State no divine or supranatural elements were necessary, because it had all the laws of its own operation within itself. . . . What generations of writers and governments had been seeking was now found in the simple application of the concept of nature. The State was, in a word, a natural thing, and herewith the conceptual gulf between it and the Church opened up. . . .
>
> . . . The State was a matter for man or the citizen only: it had neither in its origin nor in its working anything to do with ecclesiastical authority.[47]

We must be careful, in examining the texts of Aquinas to be subjected to analysis in this book, to ascertain whether this conceptual gulf is so evident in Aquinas' thought as Ullmann would have us believe.

Notwithstanding this issue, the shift in Aquinas from the conventional to the natural view of civil authority does mark, at least by implication, the detachment of philosophical analysis from theodicy with respect to the nature of that authority itself. The conventional view manifests one aspect of the theological problem of evil; it is the cry of Job turned upon the prospect of political controversy. The problem of the existence of evil in a divinely created world is one which preoccupied Augustine.[48] With respect to civil authority

---

[47]Ullman, p. 179.

[48]See, e.g., De Civitate Dei 11:16-18, 12:1-9. See generally The Encyclopedia of Philosophy, 1972 Reprint ed., s.v. "Evil, The Problem of," by John Hick.

specifically, how is it that God would subject one man to another, and worse yet, how is it that tyrants are allowed to thrive? As we shall see, the problem of civil authority is posed in precisely these terms by Lombard. The answer of the conventionalist view is that civil authority is imposed on man, not as a natural condition (for subjection and tyranny are unnatural), but as a punishment and a test in his fallen state.

The natural view rejects this solution, and civil society is taken to be a natural feature of man as man, possessing positive value. However, this development gives rise to a more specific, more particularly philosophical aspect of the problem of civil authority, what d'Entreves refers to as "the problem of political obligation."[49] It is this aspect of the problem which gives currency to the reflections of the Medieval thinkers to be considered in this analysis. Indeed, as d'Entreves argues,[50] this more specific manifestation of the problem of civil authority establishes a continuity between the philosophical problems confronting the Medieval thinkers and the seminal inquiry of the Greek philosophers. The problem involves the determination and delimitation of political obligation itself. Resolving this problem is unavoidably linked to a consideration of the nature and demands of obedience, and ultimately the nature of political authority itself. The interrelationship of these various, specific aspects of the problem of civil authority is reflected in the sententail commentaries which are the subject of this analysis. Furthermore, the emergence of this set of related issues makes the problem of civil authority, as reflected in these Medieval commentaries distinctly contemporary with our own times, in a sense in which the Patristic version of the problem is not.

---

[49]A.P. d'Entreves, The Medieval Contribution to Political Thought (London: Oxford University Press, 1939), p. 3.

[50]See ibid., pp. 4-5.

In another passage, this commentator characterizes the fundamental problem as "that of the nature and value of political experience."[51] Thus, we may identify three aspects of the "problem" of civil authority: (i) the confrontation between the conventional, Patristic view of civil authority and the rediscovered Aristotelian, natural view; (ii) the problem of evil, manifested in political terms by the subjection of man to man; and, (iii) the problem of political obligation to civil authorities generally "and," as Aquinas would emphasize, "especially tyrants."[52] It is suggested that, to a greater or lesser extent, each of these manifestations of the "problem" of civil authority turns upon one's understanding of "the sources of authority, the duty and limits of obedience"[53] to such authority.

An examination of the source of civil authority as identified within the philosophy of Aquinas must first address certain preliminary questions, questions which determine the context of the discussion. First, what is meant by the term "source"? One might argue that, in a narrow sense, the source of authority is always power, i.e., physical force or the threat thereof. For if such power is not evident, in what sense can any civil authority command? However, the narrow sense is inadequate for present purposes; civil authority claims preeminence for itself not only de facto but also de jure.[54] Therefore, for purposes of this analysis, the inquiry into the source of civil authority is a search for the answer to the question, "How is it that any civil authority can claim for itself that it acts de jure?"[55]

---

[51]Ibid., p. 20.

[52]II Scriptum super Libros Sent. 44, 2, 2.

[53]d'Entreves, Medieval Contribution, p. 31.

[54]See, e.g., Yves R. Simon, Nature and Functions of Authority (Milwaukee: Marquette University Press, 1948), p. 8, citing Summa Theologiae, I-II, Q. 95, a. 1.

[55]For a basic discussion of the concept of

This inquiry leads to a second preliminary question. What is meant by "civil authority"? The term is intended to be generic. It encompasses all that is included within the power of the state, as distinct from that of the Church, or of any informal social grouping.[56]

Third, why is an examination of the source of civil authority at all significant in any philosophical enterprise? In one sense, such an examination is significant because it is logically prior to an examination of what follows from the moment at which civil authority emerges: the rights and duties of those subject to it. However, the examination is also significant in terms of influencing the direction that the philosophical enterprise will take. It is the present writer's view that the choice made by a philosopher in answering the question of the source of civil authority is the analytic key to his entire political philosophy as it subsequently unfolds. The reason for this is that the source of that authority is the ground upon which the legitimacy of its exercise will be judged. Naturally enough, the determination made concerning the source of authority will dictate certain limitations in the relationship between the authority and its subjects.

---

authority, its nature, source and limits, see Simon, note 54, supra. See also S. I. Benn, "The Uses of Sovereignty," Political Studies 3 (1955):109-22; C. W. Cassinelli, "Political Authority: Its Exercise and Possession," Western Political Quarterly 14 (1961):635-46; S. de Grazia, "What Authority is Not," American Political Science Review 53 (1959):321-31. See generally The Encyclopedia of Philosophy, 1972 Reprint ed., s.v. "Authority," by Stanley I. Benn; R. S. Peters, P. G. Winch and A. E. Duncan-Jones, "Symposium: Authority," Proceedings of the Aristotelian Society 32 (Supplementary Volume, 1958):207-60.

[56]In this sense, the term is meant to correspond to the term potestas saeculara as used by Aquinas in the sentential commentary. See, e.g., II Scriptum super Libros Sent. 44, 2, 2: Utrum Christiani teneantur obedire potestatibus saecularibus, et maxime tryannis.

Furthermore, the relationship between Aquinas' political theory and his overriding theological perspective may also be revealed in the problem of obedience to civil authority. The problem develops on several levels. First, can the two perspectives of Aristotelianism and the Patristic tradition of Christianity be reconciled in a political philosophy? For example, in his sentential commentary Aquinas addresses the question of whether Christians are required to obey secular powers. If faith gives freedom, if a greater bond has now been accepted by the believer, then can the Christian still be bound to obey the secular authority? This argument in effect rehearses the problem of civil authority as it manifests the underlying theological problem of the existence of evil. Aquinas' reply will link the obedience to the power with the authority of the precept which the power pronounces.

He will argue that

> obedience looks to the obligation of observing in the command which is served. However, this duty is caused by the order of a sovereignty which possesses constraining force, not only temporally but also spiritually as a matter of conscience, . . . insofar as the order of sovereignty derives from God. . . . And thus, as to what comes from God, the Christian is required to obey such people, but not insofar as a sovereignty which is not from God.[57]

The problem of civil authority, of its source and its limits, was to be a continuing theme in Aquinas' comments on political themes. It is at the center of the sentential commentary on Distinction 44. It appears prominently in those sections of the Summa dealing with issues of legal philosophy.[58] It

---

[57]II Scriptum super Libros Sent. 44,2,2, Solutio.

[58]It is only possible in the broadest sense, of course, that we can refer to the "political thought" of Aquinas. "To treat St. Thomas' political theory

will continue to be problematic in such tracts as <u>De regimine principum</u>, addressed to the King of Cyprus.[59]

The task for Aquinas is to posit a concept of civil authority which is capable of resolving the apparently conflicting demands upon the believer/subject imposed by <u>rex</u> and <u>sacerdos</u>. First, however, it is necessary to examine in detail the text upon which Aquinas was commenting when he initially encountered the problem of civil authority.

This text, Lombard's <u>Sentences</u>, defined the specific context in which the problem made its appearance on the horizon of Acquinas' thought.

II. THE PROBLEM OF CIVIL AUTHORITY IN LOMBARD'S SENTENCES

Peter Lombard consolidates his remarks on the problem of civil authority in one small section out of three in Distinction 44 of Book Two of his <u>Sentences</u>.[60] At first glance, it would appear that the first two sections of the distinction have little, if anything, to do with that problem. However, there is a significant connection between the first two sections of Distinction 44, dealing with the human potential for sin, and the final section, dealing with the problem of civil authority.

---

as a separate field of study is almost as artificial as it is to treat St. Augustine's as such. . . . [Aquinas'] remarks on the social and political order have to be extracted from the main structure of his philosophical and theological works." Morrall, p. 70. In a sense, the rediscovery (and assimilation) of Artistotle creates the political category.

[59]See particularly Chapter IV of the <u>De regimine principum</u>, on the problem of the duty owed to a tyrant.

[60]A translation of Distinction 44 is set forth in Part I, infra.

The material compiled by Lombard in this distinction did not uniformly engage the attention of sentential commentators. Some, more or less confining themselves to the problem of the human potential for sin, disposed of the distinction in but a few pages of their respective commentaries.[61] However, other sentential commentators, including Aquinas and Bonaventure, seem to have had their attention dramatically engaged by the issues raised by Distinction 44.[62] We may take this fact as a recommendation for further study of Lombard's text.

Distinction 44 in its Context within the "Sentences"

Let us place this distinction in its context in Book Two of Lombard's Sentences. That context is essentially theological in its concerns. This fact should not be surprising, since Lombard was by

---

[61] For example, Duns Scotus frames his commentary on the distinction in a single question, Utrum potentia peccandi sit a Deo? He then disposes of the question in less than three printed pages. See John Duns Scotus, Commentaria Oxoniensia ad IV Libros Magistri Sententiarum, ed. M. Fernandez Garcia, 2 vols. (Florence: Typographia Collegii S. Bonaventurae, 1914), 2:909-11. Similarly, Alexander of Hales devotes scarcely four printed pages to the distinction. See Alexander of Hales, Glossa in quatuor Libros Sententiarum, part II: In Librum Secundum, Bibliotheca Franciscana Scholastica Medii Aevi, vol. XIII (Florence: Typographia Collegii S. Bonaventurae, 1952), pp. 417-20.

[62] See, e.g., Aquinas' commentary on this distinction, which occupies over twenty printed pages. Thomas Aquinas, Scriptum Super Libros Sententiarum Magistri Petri Lombardi Episcopi Parisiensis, ed. R.P. Mandonnet, 3 vols. (Paris: P. Lethielleux, 1929), 2:1114-36. A translation of this portion of Aquinas' sentential commentary is set forth in Part II, infra. Bonaventure's sentential commentary also devotes twenty printed pages to this distinction. Bonaventure, Opera Theologica Selecta Vol. 2: Sententiarum Liber II (Florence: Typographia Collegii S. Bonaventure, 1938), pp. 1040-59. For a translation see infra Part III.

profession and repute a theologian.[63] The four books of the <u>Sentences</u> divide neatly among them the following respective subjects: (i) the Trinity and the attributes of God; (ii) creation and sin; (iii) the mystery of the Incarnation of Christ as man, the life of grace, and the virtues; and, (iv) the sacraments and the "Last Things."[64]

Distinction 44 is the last distinction to appear in Book Two of the Sentences. It is immediately preceded by two distinctions concerned with the nature of sin itself.[65]

---

[63]Father Brady has noted, "By 1142 [Lombard] was known as a 'celebrated theologian,' and in the same year Gerhoh of Reichersberg mentions his gloss on St. Paul. . . ." <u>The Encyclopedia of Philosophy</u>, 1972 Reprint ed., s.v. "Peter Lombard," by Ignatius Brady.

[64]See, e.g., Hinrich Stoevesandt, <u>Die Letzten Dinge in der Theologie Bonaventuras</u> (Zurich: EVZ-Verlag, 1969).

[65]Distinction 42 is concerned with the following questions about the nature of sin:
"An voluntas et actio mala in eodem homine et circa eamdem rem sint unum peccatum vel plura.
-- Si peccatum ab aliquo admissum in eo sit quousque poeniteat.
-- Quibus modis dicitur in Scriptura reatus.
-- De modis peccatorum, qui multipliciter assignantur.
-- Quomodo differant delictum et peccatum.
-- De septem vitiis principalibus.
-- De superbia, quae est radix omnis mali.
-- Quo sensu utrumque dicatur radix omnium malorum, scilicet superbia et cupiditas."
Distinction 43 is concerned with the following questions about the act of sin:
"De peccato in Spiritum sanctum, quod dicitur etiam peccatum ad mortem.
-- Quid sit illud peccatum.
-- An omnis obstinatio vel desperatio peccatum sit Spiritum sanctum.
-- Quod aliter accipitur peccatum in Spiritum sanctum.
-- Alia assignatio peccati in Spiritum sanctum."

Unlike those preceding distinctions, which present a relatively lengthly series of questions, Distinction 44 presents only three issues. The first two explicitly concern the potential for sin: (i) De potentia peccandi, an sit homini vel diabolo a Deo; and, (ii) Auctoritatem astruit, potentiam peccandi esse a Deo. These issues in effect raise one aspect of the theological dilemma of the existence of evil in a divinely created universe. Though he does not touch upon a direct formulation of this dilemma (e.g., how it could be possible that God would create a world in which evil and suffering exist, and even appear to triumph), Lombard assembles Patristic opinions (sententiae) on the underlying question of the source of the potential for sin. Does it come from God? If not, how can evil persist? If so, is God vicariously responsible for acts of sin arising from that potential?

Following these two issues, Lombard's text then raises what may seem to be a non sequitur. The third issue included in Distinction 44 directly concerns one aspect of the problem of civil authority, namely, the permissibility vel non of resistance to civil authority: An aliquando resistendum sit potestati. One interpretive problem with respect to the text is, therefore, whether there is a coherent analytical relationship between this last issue and the first two. In other words, is there any significant sense in which the question of resistance to civil authority relates to the issue of the persistence of evil in a divinely created world? This relationship may give some indication of Lombard's attitude towards the status of civil authority itself.

It should also be noted that Distinction 44 serves a transitional function in the overall structure of the Sentences. The transition from the preceding two distinctions is straightforward enough. Having been primarily concerned throughout Book Two with theological problems surrounding creation, the fall of man and the nature of sin, Lombard understandably turns his attention to the persistence of the potential for sin. In his "Literal Exposition" of this text, Aquinas has occasion to impose an Aristotelian gloss on this transition in discourse from act of sin to potential for sin. He argues that this transition illustrates the Aristotelian principle that, historically and pedagogically, we come to know the potential from our knowledge of the act.[66] Aquinas observes that the order of the transition (from act to potency) is to be accounted for in the following way:

> The reason for the order here is: because the potential is known through the act. Therefore, the determination of the act of sin must be prior to that of the potential for sin, although the potential is prior in itself to the act.[67]

Aquinas' application of an Aristotelian methodology to his task as a sentential commentator is admirably complete. He not only explains the literal order of the text in terms of the priority of act in the order of knowledge, but also appends a passing note indicating the obverse principle, the relative priority of potentiality in itself.[68]

It goes almost without saying that this gloss is entirely gratuitous, at least for a "literal exposition" of this text by a commentator. While it may further the project of assimilating Aristotelianism into orthodox medieval philosophy,[69]

---

[66]Cf. Metaphysics, Book 19, Chapter 8, 1049^{b}14-18.

[67]Aquinas, II Scriptum super Libros Sent., Expositio Textus.

[68]The question of the relation of prior/posterior between act and potential in Aristotle is not without its ambiguity. See, e.g., Metaphysics 1019^{a}8-11, where Aristotle discusses the senses in which some objects are prior "with respect to potentiality, others with respect to actuality." In principle, however, actuality is prior to potentiality in formula, in substance and in time. See ibid., 1049^{b}11-12.

[69]This "project" was one in which Aquinas was the primary moving force, not simply in relation to political philosophy, but across the spectrum of philosophical concerns. See generally, D. T. Mullane, "Aristotelianism in St. Thomas" (Ph.D.

it is extraneous to the narrow task of preparing a commentary, let alone a "literal exposition" of Lombard's text. That text is certainly not "Aristotelian," in content or purpose, nor is it even intended primarily to be "philosophical."

Nevertheless, Distinction 44 does provide a transition from the earlier discussion of the act of sin to a consideration of the potential for sin. Aquinas recognizes this fact, and he provides an explanation for the order of the transition which is consistent with Aristotelian principles. His gloss thus demonstrates both that the project of assimilation was fully in progress at this early stage in his career, and that the assimilation was so thorough as to include even such specialized methodological concerns as are illustrated in the passage just quoted.

Naturally, Bonaventure does not appear to share any interest in applying Aristotelian methodology to the textual analysis of Lombard's compilation. Like Aquinas, he notes the transition taking place at the beginning of Distinction 44, but he gives no methodological gloss to the text:

> Previously the Master [i.e., Lombard] indicated how sin has its beginning in the will, in general and in particular. In this part [i.e., Distinction 44] he determines wherein the potential for sin has its beginning, continuing to the end of the book.[70]

---

dissertation, The Catholic University of America, 1929), p. 52. John B. Morrall, *Political Thought in Medieval Times* (New York: Harper Torchbooks, 1962), p. 70. Of course, the project most emphatically included the assimilation of Aristotelian principles of political philosophy. *Ibid.*, p. 68. See also Jean Dunbabin, "Aristotle in the Schools," in *Trends in Medieval Political Thought*, ed. Beryl Smalley (Oxford: Basil Blackwell, 1965), pp. 65-85.

[70]Bonaventure, *Liber II Sent.* 44, *Divisio Textus*.

The distinction also contains a transition from Book Two, which concludes with Distinction 44, to Book Three, which concerns the Incarnation, grace and the virtues. One might speculate that Lombard was anxious to pass to these new subjects. The transitional passage at the end of the distinction is abrupt and cryptic:

> Until now we directed the entire attention of the mind to these thoughts and studies which pertain to the mystery of the Word incarnate, so that we may be able to say at least some little bit about ineffable matters, thanks to God's revelation.[71]

In the textual analyses of their respective commentaries, Aquinas and Bonaventure dispose of this passage as a mere transitional device. Aquinas views the passage as the beginning of a new part of the Sentences which Lombard "continues into the following book. . . ."[72] Bonaventure also views the passage as entirely separable from the main discussion of the distinction, and he betrays perhaps a certain annoyance with the formalities of Lombard's style:

> The Master continues the discourse, so that it passes from this book to the third one, at the place where he says, "Until now we directed the entire attention of the mind," and so forth. This last small section could be separated from the whole preceding part, but on account of its brevity it has not been divided off. In this way, therefore, the details of the divisions [of the distinction] are more a matter of curiosity than utility, and for that reason I have passed over them. . . .[73]

---

[71]Lombard, Liber II Sent. 44.

[72]Aquinas, II Scriptum super Libros Sent. 44, Divisio Textus.

[73]Bonaventure, supra note 70.

These details aside, however, it should be clear that the context in which the distinction is placed is decidedly theological.

Textual Analysis of Distinction 44

This distinction is divided into three sections.[74] In the first, Lombard frames the problem of the potential for sin, namely, does this potential arise in man or the devil from God.[75] That Lombard includes the reference to the devil in this statement of the question suggests that he is concerned not with some exercise in philosophical anthropology, but rather with an aspect of the traditional theological problem of the existence (or the persistence) of evil in a divinely created world.[76] The question is, in Lombard's view, "worthy of consideration."[77] Behind the question stands the issue of whether it is conceivable that a purportedly benevolent God could be the source of the world's capacity for evil and misery.

In the passages of his text in which he makes a presentation of the question, however, Lombard confines himself to a discussion of the human potential for sin. So, for example, the text of this section rephrases the question as follows: "whether the potential for sin arises in us from God or from ourselves."[78] The devil is then introduced in the discussion as yet another possible source of the human potential for sin.

Lombard's analysis of the alternative answers to the question does relate back, indirectly at least, to his discussion of the will and the act of

---

[74]There are four sections, if one includes the transitional paragraph at the end of the distinction.

[75]See Lombard, supra note 71.

[76]For a discussion of the traditional problem of evil, see text at note 48, supra.

[77]Lombard, supra note 71.

[78]Ibid., (emphasis added).

sin in Distinction 42. He notes that one could argue that, by analogy to the bad will which arises from ourselves or from the devil, but not from God, the potential for good may come from God but not the potential for evil. Thus, Lombard concludes his presentation of the problem of the source of the potential for sin in the following way:

> [N]either man nor angel can possess the morally good will from himself, but only the bad. Similarly, concerning the potential for good and evil, others say (by way of metaphor to the will) that the former comes from God, but not the latter.[79]

It is important to recognize that this passage constitutes only an exposition by Lombard of the problem, not necessarily a statement of Lombard's (or the orthodox Patristic) view of the resolution of the problem. Both Aquinas and Bonaventure stress this point in their respective commentaries. Aquinas describes the structure of Lombard's text in this regard as follows:

> [Lombard] makes three points. First, he puts forward the question. Second, he relates certain opinions. . . . Third, he determines the truth.[80]

As Aquinas identifies the pertinent passages of the text, only the first and second points are included in the portion which we have so far considered. Similarly, Bonaventure notes that in the first portion of the text, Lombard only "determines that, in the opinion of some, the potential for sin is not from God."[81]

It is not until the second section of the distinction that Lombard in effect presents his own

---

[79]Ibid.

[80]Aquinas, supra note 72 (emphasis added).

[81]Bonaventure, supra note 70 (emphasis added).

view by marshalling a compilation of scriptural passages and opinions of the Fathers in support of the proposition that "the power for evil comes from God, from whom all power comes."[82] He begins with a quotation from Romans 13:1, "There is no authority[83] except from God," which, Lombard asserts, should be read as referring to "not only the power for good, but also for evil."[84] Similarly, Lombard cites the colloquy between Christ and Pilate, in which the former is said to assert that Pilate would have no power if it had not been given "from above".[85]

The remainder of Lombard's pertinent authorities are Augustine,[86] the Old Testament and Gregory.[87] The Old Testament sources relate directly to the dilemma of the existence of evil and misery in a divinely created world. Not surprisingly, quotations from Job figure prominently here.[88] Lombard apparently seeks to resolve the dilemma by adopting the "Augustinian" view that the conventions of society, exposing people to evil and misery, are to

---

[82]Lombard, supra note 71.

[83]"Authority" here is a translation of *potestas*. The terminology in this regard is somewhat ambiguous and capable of many shades of meaning. See, e.g., Part II, note 3, infra.

[84]Lombard, supra note 71.

[85]John 19:11.

[86]Lombard cites Augustine's *On the Psalms*, 32:3, for the proposition that the desire, but not the power, to be harmful is internal to man's wickedness. The power must be "given".

[87]*In Moralibus*, 26:26.

[88]Lombard refers to Job 2:5 (wherein the devil entreats the Lord, "Put forth your hand") and Job 34:30 ("He makes the hypocrite to reign on account of the sins of the people"). Other passages cited by Lombard are Proverbs 8:15-16 and Hosea 13:11, each supporting the notion that it is God who is directly responsible for the imposition of tyrants upon the people.

be endured as an instrument of divine retribution and cleansing.[89] In one of the few direct assertions by Lombard, we have a fairly unembellished apologia for this subtle instrument:

> Certainly, the will for wickedness can come from the spirit of man. Yet there is no power except from God, and this is a secret and fitting justice. Through the power given to the devil, God performs his own just deeds. . . . [T]here is no power for good or evil . . . except from the impartial God, even if the impartiality may be unknown to you.[90]

Are we to conclude, therefore, that Lombard's "Augustinian" apologia for the misery encountered in this world requires uncritical endurance of the travail of history? Lombard's reply to this question would illustrate the danger of applying a characterization like that implied by the term "Augustinian" as a generalization. Lombard's admittedly Augustinian orientation in fact does not counsel uncritical acceptance of travail in earthly existence, for such an existence involves action and choice, raising the possibility of moral crisis.

In fact, the third section of the distinction raises just such an issue, one "which cannot be passed over in silence."[91] If the power for evil is a subtle instrument of God, then can one ever rightly resist such a power? Lombard approaches

---

[89]It is of course dangerous to generalize and identify as "Augustinian" this notion of secular authority as a convention divinely imposed as a retribution. Nevertheless, the "conventional" view, perhaps more safely identified as a "Patristic" notion, was the received view until the resurgence of Aristotle. See, e.g., Walter Ullmann, A History of Political Thought: The Middle Ages (Baltimore: Penguin Books, 1968), pp. 122-3; Morrall, Political Thought, pp. 68-9.

[90]Lombard, supra note 71.

[91]Ibid.

this issue by introducing a "worst case" analysis, which we may paraphrase in the following terms:

(i) We have accepted the view that no power,[92] for good or evil, exists except insofar as it is give to man or the devil by God.

(ii) Looking at Romans 13:2, however, we find the admonition, "He who resists authority[93] has resisted the ordinance of God."

(iii) However, in applying this admonition to the view accepted in (i), supra, we seem to be compelled to the conclusion that we ought not to resist the power of the devil.

Thus, the positing of this "worst case" illustrates one aspect of the critical dilemma presented by the persistence of the potential for evil. It should be noted that Lombard does not proceed through the analysis as a reductio ad absurdum.[94] The dilemma is resolved not by

---

[92]We lose some of the ambiguity of the problem raised by Lombard in this section in the Latin original. At this point in his text, he uses the term potestas ("power"), instead of potentia ("power," "potential"), as used in framing the question in the first section of the distinction. This seemingly slight change in terminology is striking in the present context, because potestas is also the term used in the admonition from Romans 13:2 which Lombard quotes in the second step of the analysis here.

[93]Potestati in the original. Cf. note 92, supra.

[94]See generally, The Encyclopedia of Philosophy, 1972 Reprint ed., s.v., "Glossary of Logical Terms," by Baruch A. Brody; idem, Logic Theoretical and Applied (Englewood Cliffs, N.J.: Prentice Hall, Inc., 1973), pp. 101, 121. Cf. George Grote, Aristotle (New York: Arno Press, 1973), p. 155.

repudiating step (iii) as an absurd conclusion, but rather by equivocating the intent of the admonition in step (ii):

> it is known that [St. Paul in Romans 13:2] was speaking of secular authority, evidently of the king, the prince and the like, <u>to whom there is to be no resistance</u> in what God commands to be rendered to them. . . .[95]

In this way, Lombard resolves the dilemma in its worst case. There remains, then, the relatively narrow question of whether there may be resistance to secular authority. Lombard has already prepared the way for his answer in the underscored portion of the above quotation. The limits of civil authority, or conversely the range of permissible resistance to that authority, remain essentially a matter of a divinely ordered convention. Civil authority is a function of "what God commands to be rendered to" those in authority. Beyond that, their writ does not run. Hence, relying solely and explicitly upon the authority of Augustine, Lombard concludes:

> If in fact some prince . . . commanded or counselled something contrary God, then that is to be resisted. . . . In doing this we do not resist the ordinance of God, but conform to it. For thus God ordained that we must obey no authority in evil.[96]

Having resolved in this fashion the dilemma of the persistence of the potential for evil, Lombard does not, unfortunately, offer any specific guidance as to the limits of civil authority. Since the dilemma is for him primarily of theological significance, it seems to be a matter of considerably less urgency to reflect upon the philosophical issues concerning the relation between civil authority and those subject to that authority.

---

[95] Lombard, supra note 71 (emphasis added).

[96] Ibid.

The Problem of Civil Authority within the Context of Distinction 44

From Lombard's point of view, the problem of civil authority seems to be simply part of the impedimenta of the theological problem of the persistence of evil. In the preceding textual analysis, we have seen how the question of the permissible resistance to authority (diabolical or human) devolves from the question of the source of the potential for sin.

It may be argued, however, that from a philosophical perspective the problem of civil authority and the problem of the potential for evil are correlative. In a sense, the theological and philosophical concerns are simply alternative versions of the one and same problem confronting the individual. If this is so, then there is nothing arbitrary about Lombard's inclusion of at least some treatment of the philosophical problem within the essentially theological setting of Distinction 44.

The key to this implicit relationship between the theological and philosophical concerns may be found in the nature of the textual authority upon which Lombard draws for support. In his discussion of the theological problem in the second section of the distinction, Lombard cites and quotes from Romans 13:1. In his discussion of the philosophical problem in the third section of the distinction, he cites and quotes Romans 13:2. These two citations form part of a text which is the <u>locus classicus</u> for medieval political philosophy. It will be useful to examine this text in its entirety:

> Let every person be in subjection to the governing authorities. For there is no authority except from God, and those which exist are established by God.
>
> Therefore he who resists authority has opposed the ordinance of God; and they who have opposed will receive condemnation upon themselves.
>
> For rulers are not a cause of fear for good behavior, but for evil. Do you want to have no fear of autho-

> rity? Do what is good, and you will have praise from the same;
>
> For it is a minister of God to you for good. But if you do what is evil, be afraid; for it does not bear the sword for nothing; for it is a minister of God, an avenger who brings wrath upon the one who practices evil.
>
> Wherefore it is necessary to be in subjection, not only because of wrath, but also for conscience's sake.
>
> For because of this you also pay taxes, for rulers are servants of God, devoting themselves to this very thing.
>
> Render to all what is due them: tax to whom tax is due; custom to whom custom; fear to whom fear; honor to whom honor.[97]

For the medieval mind the problem of civil authority raised "first and foremost . . . if not in actually promoting theoretical developments, certainly in stirring the deepest emotional reactions, . . . the religious issue."[98] In an earlier, and perhaps simpler, age, the conventional, Patristic view of civil authority could confine the scope of political obligation. Political institutions were conventional institutions imposed by God as a result of human corruption and sin.[99] Political institu-

----

[97]Romans 13:1-7.

[98]A.P. d'Entreves, The Medieval Contribution, p. 7.

[99]"[I]n their explanation of the state as a system of organized force, the Christian writers could lay the greatest possible stress upon an idea which . . . only found its direct confirmation in dogma and biblical teaching: the idea of human corruption and sinfulness. Thus Christian political

tions if not sinful, had their origin in sin.[100] Hence, the problem of civil authority was, in a sense, a theological issue. That being so, the text from Romans quoted above was of obvious significance. Indeed, as one commentator on this period has noted, "the whole history of Christian political theory can well be said to be nothing else than an uninterrupted commentary upon this text."[101] We hasten to add to that statement, "at least until the resurgence of Aristotle."

Given this conventional view of the nature of political obligation, therefore, the problem of civil authority is indeed a religious issue. Hence, the problem does not simply follow from the problem of the potential for evil, as is evident from Lombard's argumentation. Rather, it is an integral part of the latter problem. This fact is implicit in Lombard's use of Romans 13 in treating each of the problems in turn. Unfortunately, as we have seen in analyzing Lombard's text, he gives virtually no independent consideration to the issues raised by the problem of civil authority beyond its theological implications. In this regard he neglects the "human issue" in the service of the religious one. Such a neglect renders impossible any separable philosophical reflection on the problem. The question remains whether the sentential commentators were able to bridge this lacuna. Such a bridge is essential to the development of political philosophy. Rational inquiry is necessary here, for ultimately

> The problem of political obligation was thus felt to involve not only a

---

philosophers . . . stressed the character of the state as a conventional but necessary institution, as a divinely appointed *poena et remedium peccati.*" Ibid., p. 15.

[100]Cf. R.W. & A.J. Carlyle, <u>A History of Mediaeval Political Theory in the West</u>, vol. III: <u>Political Theory from the Tenth Century to the Thirteenth</u>, (New York: Barnes & Noble, Inc., 1928), p. 182.

[101]A.P. d'Entreves, p. 9.

religious, but a purely human issue: an issue, that is, which required to be faced not only by appealing to faith, but by resorting to criticism, in order to explain the existence of political institutions and their value in relation to the nature and destiny of man. It is for this purpose that medieval thought endeavored to construct a theory of politics not only upon a religious, but upon a philosophical and legal basis.[102]

Reflection upon the sentential commentaries of Aquinas and Bonaventure will demonstrate that they were aware of the ambiguities and vulnerabilities inherent in Lombard's use of sources such as Romans 13. It may be argued that this awareness, at a relatively early stage in their repective careers, may indicate at least the motivation behind the movement in later medieval philosophy towards more specific inquiry into the "human issue."

In his "Literal Exposition" at the end of his commentary on Distinction 44, Aquinas clearly identifies the ambiguity of Lombard's use of certain textual authorities (including Romans 13) in his theological discussion of the potential for sin in the second section of the distinction. Lombard asserts at the beginning of this section that "it has been shown beyond doubt by the witness of many holy men that the power for evil comes from God."[103] Aquinas notes:

It seems that this proof of the Master may be of no use at all. This is so because the authorities which follow [i.e., those which Lombard then cites] are not speaking of the potential for sin, but of the power of sovereignty.[104]

---

[102]Ibid., p. 13.

[103]Lombard, supra note 71.

[104]Aquinas, II Scriptum super Libros Sent. 44, Expositio.

In an apparent allusion to the conventional view of the role of civil authority (i.e., the divine punishment of the sovereign's subjects through the unwitting instrument of the sovereign), Aquinas seems willing to allow Lombard's use of these textual authorities for his "proof." The weakness of Lombard's argumentation in this regard is again cited by Aquinas, however, when he considers the critical step in Lombard's argument at which the latter confines Romans 13 to secular authority.[105] Aquinas questions the adequacy of Lombard's resolution of the "worst case" dilemma:

> It seems that this solution of the Master is insufficient. This is so because earlier he showed that even the power for doing evil which the devil possesses is from God, and thus it seems that, if one is to obey a power because it comes from God, then the devil is to be obeyed. But it is said without a doubt that the authority of [St. Paul in Romans 13] is to be understood only concerning the power of sovereignty. The devil does not have power of whatever kind over men. . . . Hence, it is not proper that all power that comes from God be obeyed, but only that power which has been established by God for this, that the obedience due to itself is laid out. The power of sovereignty is alone that way.[106]

Thus, Aquinas criticizes the inadequacy of Lombard's argumentation with respect to the problem of civil authority. By stressing that Romans 13 and similar texts are distinguishable from considerations of the theological problem of the persistence of evil, Aquinas may be giving greater emphasis to the independent philosophical problem of the nature and limits of civil authority. It is this problem,

---

[105]See text at notes 92-95, supra.

[106]Aquinas, II *Scriptum super Libros Sent.* 44, Expositio.

whatever its theological underpinnings, which is at issue in Romans 13, and it is this problem which is at the heart of the "human issue." As we have seen in Aquinas' criticism of Lombard's resolution of the dilemma, Aquinas emphasizes that the intrinsic character of sovereignty itself explains the fact that civil authority is legitimate.

Having himself asserted that the power of sovereignty is in some sense *sui generis*, it is incumbent upon Aquinas to initiate a rational inquiry into the nature and limits of civil authority. This he does in the course of his sentential commentary.[107] We shall have occasion to examine the results of that inquiry later in this introduction.[108]

Bonaventure identifies much the same vulnerabilities in Lombard's argumentation, in a concluding section of his commentary on Distinction 44 entitled "Doubts concerning the Writings of the Master." First and foremost he questions Lombard's resolution of the dilemma by confining Romans 13 to secular authority. In this regard Bonaventure notes that

> it does not appear that the Master sufficiently resolved the question presented. To the contrary, he avoids it, since . . . the devil does not possess the power to do evil from himself but from God. When therefore [St. Paul, in Romans 13] says that "All power is from God," he understood not only the power of man, but also that of the devil.[109]

---

[107]See ibid., 44,1,2 (*Utrum omnis praelatio sit a Deo*); 44,1,3 (*Utrum in statu innocentiae fuisset dominium*); 44,2,2 (*Utrum Christiani teneantur obedire potestatibus saecularibus, et maxime tyrannis*).

[108]See text at notes 115-223, infra.

[109]Bonaventure, *Liber II Sent.* 44, *Dubium*.

Note that, unlike Aquinas, Bonaventure is not yet willing to concede to Lombard even the proposition that Romans 13 is concerned only with secular authority. Having presented this basic question, Bonaventure elaborates on the problem by adding the following subtlety. If one assumes <u>arguendo</u> that the dilemma is unresolved (i.e., that the God-given power of the devil cannot be resisted), then it follows that

> Likewise, we ought not resist the power of the devil's agents, namely, evil prelates and tyrants who are agents of the devil.[110]

In responding to the questions he has raised, Bonaventure is finally willing to accept the view that Romans 13 "is to be understood as concerning human authority, not diabolic authority."[111] However, his reason for accepting this view is founded upon his conception of authority, not (like Lombard) upon simple exegesis of St. Paul's text. True authority depends upon the orderly relationship between those invested with authority and those who are subject to that authority. Human authority, at least in principle, "is both ordained and frequently moves and commands in an orderly manner."[112] Diabolic "authority" (which is in fact only "power") is in contrast always disordered and perverse, and hence is to be resisted. Note, however, that on the basis of this conceptual resolution of Lombard's dilemma, the problem of the authority of evil prelates and tyrants "is not the same"[113] as the problem of diabolic "authority" and is not therefore capable of the same conceptual resolution. In other words, while the authority of evil prelates and tyrants may be aberrant, it is nevertheless in principle still authority. Such pathological instances of human authority are, again at least in

---

[110]<u>Ibid.</u>

[111]<u>Ibid.</u>

[112]<u>Ibid.</u>

[113]<u>Ibid.</u>

principle, still ordained. Hence the problem of civil authority, as a "human issue," remains even after the resolution of the underlying "religious issue."

Whatever our assessment of the merits of Lombard's writings, several important aspects of the place of the problem of civil authority may be gleaned from Lombard's treatment and the reaction of his commentators. It may be inferred that, for Lombard, the problem of the nature and the limits of civil authority is a mere appendage of the broader theological problem of the persistence of evil in the world. This aspect may be inferred both from his invocation of many of the same textual authorities in his discussion of each problem, and from his facile resolution of the dilemma of the application of Romans 13 to the problem of the persistence of evil. Once that fundamentally theological issue has been resolved, the related problem of civil authority is disposed of with virtually no discussion.

Nevertheless, Lombard's commentators appear to recognize that his treatment of the two problems is not satisfactory. Both Aquinas and Bonaventure note that the citation of Romans 13 in the context of the theological problem is not entirely appropriate. Corresponding to this inadequacy is the fact that a treatment of Romans 13 in the context of the philosophical problem, in each of their respective views, has not been sufficiently developed by Lombard. Each commentator is impelled to elaborate upon the latter problem in his sentential commentary on Distinction 44, superficially out of proportion to Lombard's own treatment of the issue.[114]

Aquinas and Bonaventure arrive at similar assessments of the nature of civil authority, albeit by somewhat different paths. Neither is content to dismiss the problem of civil authority when the resolution of the underlying theological problem of the persistence of evil has been achieved. Both deem the issue worthy of its own analysis, and both

---

[114]Other sentential commentators apparently parallelled more closely Lombard's own relative lack of interest in the subject of the nature and limits of civil authority. Cf. note 61, supra.

appear to indicate that resolution of this issue requires an inquiry into the nature of authority in itself. Tentatively, we have seen that for Aquinas the power of sovereignty, unlike any other power, is such that it is established ("ordained") by God and is appropriate in itself for obedience. Consequently, Romans 13 requires that civil authority be respected. Bonaventure also recognizes the importance of the nature of civil authority taken in itself. The notion of order is essential to his conception of authority, and specificially, the orderly relationship between governed and governing. Hence, on principle civil authority is distinguishable from diabolical power.

Nevertheless, these conceptions are only tentative indications of the initiation of rational inquiry beyond Lombard's brief comments on the problem of civil authority. We must still see how the two sentential commentators fill out their respective conceptions of civil authority. Furthermore, we must examine their attempts to resolve the "human issue," the permissible resistance to specific civil authorities, once obedience to civil authority in the abstract has been accepted on principle.

III. AQUINAS' SENTENTIAL COMMENTARY

The Structure of the Commentary on Distinction 44

The starting point of Aquinas' first treatment of the problem of civil authority is Lombard's Distinction 44 in Book II of the Sentences, and the structure of Aquinas' commentary may be expected to follow, at least nominally, the structure of the distinction itself. However, while formally deferring to the structure of the "subject" of his commentary, Aquinas will greatly expand the range of questions which he organizes under the skeletal format of Lombard's distinction.[115] Hence, it may

---

[115]This sort of wholesale expansion of the number and scope of questions considered under the topics raised by Lombard's Sentences was already a common practice at the time Aquinas wrote his

be useful to begin this analysis of Aquinas' sentential commentary with an examination of its internal structure, for two reasons. First, since the structure of the commentary is not simply a replication of the structure of Lombard's distinction, it would be confusing to proceed to an analysis of the commentary with only the structure of the latter in mind.[116] Second, if it is true that Aquinas' sentential commentary already represents his "choices in doctrine and methodology"[117] and is characteristic of Aquinas' "originality and profoundness of thought,"[118] then it may be reasonable to assume that Aquinas' decision to depart from the structure of the subject of his commentary was itself an intentional one which may reveal something of the originality of the commentator.

Aquinas' commentary is divided into three major parts. First, he sets forth a textual analysis,[119] an extremely short, literal commentary which does little more than catalog the parts of the subject of the commentary. Second, he identifies and discusses at length two "questions"[120] which constitute the main body of the commentary. This represents Aquinas' creative work, carrying the analysis far

---

sentential commentary. These "commentaries" were no longer strictly literal. See M.-D. Chenu, Toward Understanding Saint Thomas, trans. A.-M. Landry and D. Hughes (Chicago: Henry Regnery Company, 1964), p. 267.

[116]The structure of Lombard's distinction is analyzed in text at notes 74-96, supra.

[117]Chenu, p. 264 (emphasis added).

[118]Battista Mondin, St. Thomas Aquinas' Philosophy in the Commentary to the Sentences (The Hague: Martinus Nijhoff, 1975), p. 1.

[119]Divisio Textus. See Part II, note 2, infra.

[120]Each follows the now classic structure of the quaestio, a structure also assiduously followed throughout the Summa Theologiae. For a discussion of the form of the quaestio, see Chenu, pp. 85 et seq.

beyond the four corners of Lombard's discussion. The questions follow a format now familiar to us from Aquinas' other, mature works. Each question, more a statement of a theme than a literal question, is divided into a series of articles.[121] These constitute the philosophical problems or questions to be considered. Each article consists of a series of numbered paragraphs, each setting forth arguments on one side of the problem, with citations of authorities[122] in support of each argument. With only one exception,[123] each of the articles in this portion of the commentary presents five such arguments. In each case, there follows an abbreviated statement of a position counter to that supported by the enumerated arguments (the Sed contra[124]), sometimes (but not always) with citation of authorities.[125] There follows a resolution of the argument (the Solutio[126]), in which Aquinas sets forth in discursive fashion his explanation of the problem raised by the article and then specifically answers each of the enumerated arguments at length. In general, it appears that the position suggested by the Sed contra in each case is more or less favored by the Solutio. We must nevertheless be careful to avoid assuming uncritically that the Sed contra itself is intended to present Aquinas' own

---

[121] Each article follows the form of the now classic articulus. See Chenu, pp. 93-96.

122. For a discussion of the use (or manipulation) of auctoritates in scholastic works of philosophy, see ibid., pp. 139-49.

123. See II Scriptum super Libros Sent. 44, 2, 1, 1-6.

124. See Chenu, p. 95.

125. Cf., e.g., II Scriptum super Libros Sent. 44, 1, 1, Sed contra ("Sed contra, Philosophus dicit") and ibid., 44, 1, 3, Sed contra (no authority cited).

126. In later works, the Respondeo dicendum. See Chenu, pp. 95-6.

view.[127] To the contrary, that view can only be safely located in the Solutio itself.

The third major part of this commentary is the Literal Exposition,[128] which presents an odd assortment of critical comments on the literal text of Lombard's distinction. Here Aquinas for the most part confines himself to editorial comments on the text itself, although he may explicate the text on occasion with a cross-reference to a particular discussion in the articles of the second part of the commentary.[129]

Thus, only the first and third parts actually constitute a literal commentary on Lombard's text. The second part, by far the most extended and significant, could easily stand on its own as philosophical discourse, requiring absolutely no reference to the other two parts or to Lombard's text. Indeed, the structure of this central portion of the commentary is virtually self-contained, bearing little resemblance to the internal structure of Lombard's text. That text might be represented schematically as follows:[130]

I. The Potential for Sin

    A. Statement of the Question
    B. Consideration of Opinions
    C. Determination of the Question

II. Duty of Obedience to Authority

    A. Statement of the Question
    B. Resolution of the Question

---

127. Ibid., p. 95: "The Sed contra, in itself, is the expression neither of the author's thesis nor of an argument borrowed from some authority as the foundation of his own position."

128. Expositio Textus. See Part II, notes 2 and 67, infra.

[129]See, e.g., Part II, text at note 72, infra.

[130]The scheme that follows in the text could also be a representation of Aquinas' own divisio

Contrast this straightforward and skeletal approach with the following schematic representation of the central part of Aquinas' commentary:

I. The Potential for Sin

   A. Whether the Potential for sin comes from God
   B. Whether all Sovereignty comes from God
   C. Whether Civil Power would exist in the State of Innocence

II. Obedience to Sovereigns

   A. Whether Obedience is a Virtue
   B. Whether Christians are required to obey secular Authorities
   C. Whether the Religious are required to obey their Prelates in all Things

Not only does Aquinas' approach significantly expand the framework of Lombard's text in terms of degree of detail; the order and relationship among the topics change. New (and presumably related) aspects of the problem emerge in the arrangement of the topics in Aquinas' commentary. The marked divergence, both in scope and arrangement of topics, between the text of subject and commentary can be graphically represented as follows:

Lombard	Aquinas
I A - C	I A
[II A - B]	I B
-------	I C
-------	II A
II A - B	II B
-------	II C

Even this schematic representation does not reflect the pragmatic, incidental detail that the so-called commentary is almost eleven times the

---

textus for Distinction 44. See Part II, text at notes 2-6, infra.

length of the text commented upon. Nor does it reflect the fact that, by choosing to group specific topics together in a certain order, Aquinas may be implying an intrinsic connection between these topics, as a matter of principle, which is not evident in Lombard's text.[131] Whether the structure of the commentary can be read to imply any substantive relationship among the issues discussed is a question which can only be determined by an extensive examination of the content of Aquinas' commentary.

The Substance of the Commentary

The main body of Aquinas' commentary on Distinction 44 begins with a Quaestio on the potential for sin, itself the primary topic of Lombard's text. Under this general heading, Aquinas groups three topics, each the subject of an article under the Quaestio. The first article, naturally enough, deals with the issue of whether the potential for sin comes from God. The second raises the (presumably related) issue of whether all sovereignty comes from God.[132] The third article addresses an issue which explicitly raises the conflict between the conventional and natural views of civil

---

[131] Indeed, Aquinas does go so far as to state explicitly that the two major topics treated by the "questions," namely, the potential for sin and the duty of obedience, are integral, two aspects of a single problem. "This question is two.fold: first, concerning the potential for sin; second, concerning obedience." II Scriptum super Libros Sent. 44, 1.

[132] The issue is phrased as stated above at the beginning of the second article itself. (Utrum omnis praelatio sit a Deo.) However, in the introduction to the first question, the issue is phrased in a different way, one in which the theological underpinning of the second article (and thus its relation to the first article) is even more explicit. (Cum secundum praelationis officium, adsit potestas multa peccata perpetrandi, quae nisi quis in statu praelationis esset, facere non posset; utrum etiam omnis praelatio a Deo sit. . . .)

50

authority.[133] If in fact all three of these issues are integrally related to the principal problem of the potential for sin, then it may be argued that, in Aquinas' view, the problem of civil authority is one manifestation of the problem of evil.[134]

Aquinas' treatment of the first article begins with an exposition of arguments denying that the potential for sin comes from God. Relying upon Anselm's dictum[135] that the capacity for sin neither comprises, nor is a part of freedom, the argument states that this capacity cannot be a natural potential, since all of these are directed towards the free choice of the will. It is not endowed preternaturally (through grace), since this is inconsistent with the very concept of grace. Hence, since human potentialities derived from God arise either in nature or grace, this capacity cannot arise from God.[136] Similarly, each of the remaining four arguments seek in one way or another to insulate God, whose works are thought to be

---

[133] In the third article this conflict can only be inferred, from the issue as stated: *Utrum in statu innocentiae fuisset dominium.* That the underlying issue is the conflict between the conventional and the natural views is, however, apparent from the phrasing of the issue in the general introduction to the first question: *utrum praelatio, sive dominium, sit a Deo in ordinationem naturae institutae vel in punitionem naturae corruptae.*

[134] On the broader theological issues of the problem of evil in Aquinas' philosophy, see generally Jacques Maritain, *St. Thomas and the Problem of Evil* (Milwaukee: Marquette University Press, 1942); E. E. Harris, *The Problem of Evil* (Milwaukee: Marquette University Press, 1977).

[135] See *De liberum arbitrium* 1:1.

[136] II *Scriptum super Libros Sent.* 44,1,1,1.

[137] Deuteronomy 32:4. Cf. II *Scriptum super Libros Sent.* 44,1,1,2. See also Maritain, pp. 5.19.

[138] See II *Scriptum super Libros Sent.* 44,1,1,4.

perfect,[137] from any causal relationship[138] with respect to this potential which is viewed as evil.[139] In essence, then, this line of argumentation seeks to resolve the theological problem of evil in part by denying any effective relation between God and a potential which is assumed to be itself evil. This approach may preserve the divine quality of all. good, but it may still throw into question whether he is all.powerful. (Otherwise, why would he allow this potential to exist, whatever its effective source?)

The *Sed contra* juxtaposed to this argument is particularly noteworthy. Poised against the theological concern with man's capacity for sin is an Aristotelian analysis of what it means to have a potency, for whatever purpose or object. We are told that "the Philosopher says" that the objects of potencies are correlative, so that the potential for good and for sin constitutes one potential directed at opposing objects. Hence, if the potential for good is admitted to be from God, "thus also the potential for sin."[140] The reference seems to be to the *Metaphysics*, Book 9, Chapter 9, where it is stated:

> Everything of which we say that it can do something, is alike capable of contraries, e.g. that of which we say that it can be well is the same as that which can be ill, and has both potencies at once; for the same potency is a potency of health and illness, of rest and motion, of building and throwing down, of being built and being thrown down. The capacity for contraries, then, is present at the same time. . . .[141]

Thus, the *Sed contra* suggests that the difficulty may in part involve an inadequate

---

[139]See, e.g., ibid., 44,1,1,3 and 5.

[140]Ibid., 44,1,1, *Sed contra*.

[141]*Metaphysics* 1051a5.10. Cf. Part II, note 12, infra.

understanding of the philosophical concept of potentiality. In this light, one might reevaluate the argument drawn from Boethius,[142] to the effect that, since the "use" of the potential for sin is sin, and hence evil, then the potential itself is evil. The allusion to Aristotle in the Sed contra may thus also involve the Metaphysics, Book 9, Chapter 3, in which Aristotle disputes the identification of the potency for X with the actuality of X. If this identification can be inferred from Boethius' argument, then his position is vulnerable, for

> evidently potency and actuality are different . . ., so that it is possible that a thing may be capable of being and not be, and capable of not being and yet be, and similarly with other kinds of predicate. . . .[143]

That this passage may be involved seems supported by the second paragraph of the Sed contra, which presents an argument in terms of the source of being (whatever its predicate). Aquinas writes: "Further, every being comes from God. But the potential for sin is a certain kind of being. Therefore, the potential for sin is from God."[144]

Of course, the Sed contra presents only a possible argument against the position taken in the enumerated arguments; it cannot be simply equated with the precise view endorsed by Aquinas in his Solutio. Nevertheless, his Solutio here adopts a position consistent with that suggested by the Sed contra. He argues that a "potentiality is known through its act." Hence, we may be able to infer something about the nature of this potential from the act of sin. In Aquinas' view that act is twofold, exhibiting a substance (substantia actus) and a deformity or shortcoming of the due circumstances

---

[142]De diff. Topic. 2:2. The argument appears in II Scriptum super Libros Sent. 44,1,1,5.

[143]Metaphysics 1047^{a}18.22.

[144]II Scriptum super Libros Sent. 44,1,1, Sed contra.

53

of the act (deformitas vel defectus debitarum circumstantiarum). Now, in the potential (i.e., the potential for human action, whether good or evil), one may see some correspondence between the "substance" of the act and the potential taken in itself. The latter is a principle of action, at least in the sense that, in the absence of such a potentiality, one would be "incapable" of any action at all. Aquinas adopts the theme of the Metaphysics, Book 9, Chapter 9, when he states that the potential "is likewise the principle of both action regulated by reason and that which is not. . . ."[145] Thus, the potential, taken in itself, is not the same as the act (of sin or otherwise). There is then nothing contradictory in accepting the view that our potential for acting comes from God. The defective circumstances surrounding the particular exercise of the potential for action are not supplied by God, but rather are a species of non. being, a privation of grace.[146] Hence, one may respond to the enumerated arguments first presented by the article by identifying certain equivocal uses of the term "potential". One may have simply misunderstood that the "potential," in itself, is not specific in its use for good or ill, but is simply a capability for human action directed towards either of a pair of contradictories.[147] The Aristotelian pedigree of this concept has already been noted, but Aquinas is careful to include a supporting reference to an auctoritas in a competing philosophical tradition:

> a sin may be committed through the free choice of the will, since the will is that by which a sin is committed and by which one lives properly, as Augustine says.[148]

---

[145]Ibid., 44,1,1, Solutio.

[146]Aquinas does admit the possibility, however, that "it may be said that the defect is indirectly from God, though not as something from a cause." Ibid.

[147]See ibid., 44,1,1, ad 1.

[148]Ibid. The reference is to Augustine, I

Alternatively, it is equivocal to speak of the "will" itself, when one may be referring to the potential of the will for action (the potential being a general prerequisite of action and neutral) or to the act of the will (the act, in its circumstances, being either good or ill). By the same token, the potential may sometimes be thought of in terms of the act which follows from it, but it is the specific use of the potential which is good or evil.[149]

It is in the second article of the first question that Aquinas confronts a specific aspect of the problem of civil authority for the first time. Unlike Lombard, he does not immediately address the question of the duty of obedience to authority. Rather, he begins with an underlying issue which is conceptually prior to the question of obedience, namely, whether all sovereignty comes from God. If sovereignty (i.e., civil authority) does not come from God, then there remains the task of determining what the source of the authority is. If the source is in fact no more than force, then it has, presumably, no inherent moral authority over men at all.

If, on the other hand, the authority does have its source, in some sense, from God, then a range of moral questions arises concerning the inherent nature and limits of that authority. Aquinas' division of the broad issue of civil authority into its component conceptual parts illustrates the formidable and precise nature of his scholarship. It also indicates the seriousness and independence with which he approaches the question of civil authority.

The article begins with a series of enumerated arguments supporting the proposition that all sovereignty is not from God. Not surprisingly, the arguments are theologically grounded. The discussion begins with the apparently straightforward fact that, as reported in Hosea 8:4, the Lord has said

---

Retract. 9:4. Cf. II Scriptum super Libros Sent. 44, 1, 1, ad 5.

[149]See ibid., ad 3.

"They have set up kings, but not by me."[150] All of the remaining arguments, however, rely upon one's common knowledge of the vicissitudes of sovereigns. Some have acquired their sovereignty through evil or perverse means,[151] or by usurpation,[152] and in many cases sovereignty appears to have been justly taken away from them.[153] The relationship between sovereign and subjects also appears in general to be greatly disordered; the foolish is over the wise, the sinner over the just.[154] On the basis of this sort of broadly empirical data, how could one say that such sovereigns find the source of their power in God?

It should be apparent, therefore, that these arguments raise the problem of the source of civil authority as an aspect of the broader problem of the existence of evil. In response to this problem, the first paragraph of the Sed contra recites an explicitly conventional view of civil authority:

> While it appears that the sovereignty of the good comes from God to a greater extent than that of the evil, still the sovereignties of the evil are from God: "He makes the hypocrite to reign because of the sins of the people."[155]

Nevertheless, the second paragraph of the Sed contra adopts a more philosophical approach to the problem, stressing the essential characteristic of the relationship of sovereign/subject. One may argue that a sense of the inherent value of ordered socio.political relations can be inferred from the argument. Aquinas writes:

---

[150]See ibid., 44,1,2,1.

[151]Ibid., 44,1,2,2.

[152]Ibid., 44,1,2,3, referring to Boethius, De consolatione philosophiae, Book 3.

[153]II Scriptum super Libros Sent. 44,1,2,4.

[154]Ibid., 44,1,2,5.

[155]Ibid., 44,1,2, Sed contra, quoting Job

everything which is ordered is from God, since from this very fact it is good. Yet in every sovereignty a certain order of the superior to the inferior is discovered. Therefore, every sovereignty is from God.[156]

It can never be emphasized enough that the Sed contra cannot be assumed to represent Aquinas' own position. That fact should be clear from the two parts of this Sed contra. They present two competing strategies of argumentation that one might adopt in responding to the enumerated arguments.

The first strategy is traditional and conventional in its approach. The second may be said to be at least consistent with an Aristotelian analysis, since it appears to imply an inherent value in civil authority. Nevertheless, this consistency should not be overemphasized. Neither the Sed contra nor the Solutio which follows it contains any explicit references to Aristotelian texts as auctoritates in the resolution of the problem.

In a sense, the strategy adopted by Aquinas in this Solutio is the same as the one adopted in the Solutio of the previous article. His analysis of sovereignty leads to the position that, in principle, it is good and has its source in God. Only in the circumstances of its specific exercise can it be considered evil. This analysis in fact identifies three features in the concept of sovereignty:

> the origin of sovereignty, the mode and the use. Accordingly, in certain cases, any one of these who attain sovereignty properly and exercise the act of sovereignty properly is good. But in fact, in certain cases the origin is bad, but the use is good. . . . [I]n certain cases the reverse

---

34:30.

[156]II Scriptum super Libros Sent. 44,1,2, Sed contra (emphasis added).

is true. . . . However, the mode, or form, of sovereignty is good in all cases.[157]

Thus, Aquinas favors the portion of the <u>Sed contra</u> which emphasizes the inherent nature (or form) of sovereignty, the structure of orderliness that is implied in the relation of sovereign/subject.

Hence, even where civil authority arises from the desire of the people rather than the preference of God (as in the passage from Hosea quoted in the first argument of the article), in Aquinas' view "the form of sovereignty itself is established by God."[158] The formal propriety of the relation of authority may be emphasized also to explain why sovereignty in itself is ordained, even though the sovereign may have attained his position unjustly in one respect or another.[159]

However, at this point Aquinas is not prepared to abandon the conventional view of authority. His response to the problem of the evil usurper is along traditional, Patristic lines. "[T]heir sovereignty is from God in punishment of those placed under them who deserve such a sovereign."[160] This harsh judgment of subjects oppressed by a usurper is singularly arbitrary and devoid of practical application as a principle of political philosophy.

Similarly arbitrary is his response to the problem of the apparent disorder to be found in situations in which unworthy sovereigns rule worthier subjects. He expresses once again the conventional view of authority. This sort of sovereignty

is ordained in punishment of the subjects who merit this. "He makes

---

[157]<u>Ibid</u>., 44,1,2, <u>Solutio</u>.

[158]<u>Ibid</u>., ad 1.

[159]<u>Ibid</u>., ad 2. Cf. <u>ibid</u>., ad 4.

[160]<u>Ibid</u>., ad 3.

the hypocrite to reign because of the sins of the people." And again: "I gave them a king in my anger." Whence it follows that, if every punishment comes from God, then such sovereignties are from God.[161]

The terms of the argument have already advanced to some degree from the conventional to the natural view. As a general principle, the <u>Solutio</u> accepts the view that there is inherent value and orderliness in the essential mode of authority. However, problematic cases of the exercise of authority result in a return to the conventional view in an attempt to rationalize the apparent disorder resulting from abuses of authority.

It is in the third article that Aquinas considers a question at the heart of the conventional view. In his essential nature, does man need civil authority? Here the article phrases the question as follows: "Whether in the state of innocence there was a civil power."[162] The enumerated arguments which begin the article support the proposition that civil power had no place in the state of innocence. In other words, man by nature is free, and the imposition of civil authority upon him is unnatural, purely a convention.

The position is supported principally by citations to scriptural passages and Patristic <u>auctoritates</u>. Among the former we find passages from the epistles.[163] Among the latter we find the

---

[161]<u>Ibid</u>., ad 5, quoting Job 34:30 and Hosea 13:11. These citations are included in Lombard's own discussion of the problem. See Part I, text at notes 12.13, infra.

[162]II <u>Scriptum super Libros Sent.</u> 44,1,3. The general statement at the beginning of the first question frames the present issue more precisely in terms of its significance for political philosophy: "Whether sovereignty, or civil power, comes from God as the establishment of a natural institution, or as punishment of a corrupt nature." <u>Ibid</u>., 44,1.

[163]See <u>ibid</u>., 44,1,3,4-5, quoting I Timothy 1:9 and I Corinthians 15:24, respectively.

dictum of Gregory, to the effect that "nature made all men equal,"[164] and, naturally enough, reference to Augustine's view that the subjection of man to man was introduced as a reward for sin.[165] Hence, the argument proceeds, in the absence of sin there would have been no civil power, since civil power involves subjection.

The conventional view is presented in a straightforward manner. What is of particular interest is that Aristotle is also called into service along with St. Paul in support of the argument. Aquinas writes:

> the Apostle [St. Paul] says, "The law is not laid down for the just man." But the Philosopher says that the necessity for establishing kings and other princes was to write laws having a coercive force for acts of virtue which the more persuasive discourse of wise men did not possess. Therefore, if all people had complied with the justice in which they were established, there would not have been sovereignty.[166]

---

[164] In Moralibus 21:15, quoted in II Scriptum super Libros Sent. 44,1,3,1.

[165] See generally De civitate Dei 19:15, cited in II Scriptum super Libros Sent. 44,1,3,2-3.

[166] II Scriptum super Libros Sent. 44,1,3,4. The reference to Aristotle is probably to the Nicomachean Ethics, Book 10, Chapter 9, passim. See particularly: (i) 1179^{b}4-18: "It is not enough to know, but we must try to have and use it [virtue], or try any other way there may be of becoming good. . . . [W]hile [arguments] seem to have power to encourage and stimulate the generous-minded . . . they are not able to encourage the many to nobility and goodness." (ii) 1179^{b}35-1180^{a}5: "But it is surely not enough that when they are young [men] should get the right nurture and attention; . . . we shall need laws for this as well, . . . for most people obey necessity rather than argument, and punishments rather than the sense of what is noble."

Here we see the way in which <u>auctoritates</u> could be manipulated for argumentative purposes. Even Aristotle, the acknowledged advocate of the natural view of civil authority, appears to support the conventional view that civil authority exists only as a coercive force, necessary to conform behavior springing from a corrupted nature.

In the face of this presentation of the conventional view, the <u>Sed contra</u> may seem almost trivial. With no citation of authority, the counter arguments merely point out: (i) that civil authority seems to exhibit some merit, and hence that merit at least should have been enhanced in the state of innocence; and, (ii) that even among the angels there appears to be an hierarchical arrangement, though their natures are not corrupt.[167] If the <u>Sed contra</u> has any serious bearing on the issue, it may be simply to indicate that, as had been emphasized in the second article, there does appear to be some inherent value to the notion of authority.

This approach is expanded in Aquinas' <u>Solutio</u>, which does endorse the view that civil authority would have existed in some form even in the absence of a corruption of man's nature.[168] Sacrificing the coercive aspect of civil power and still relying on Aristotle for authority, Aquinas insists upon a positive value for civil power:

(iii) 1180^{a}21-25: "The law has compulsive power, while it is at the same time a rule proceeding from a sort of practical wisdom and reason. And while people hate men who oppose their impulses, even if they oppose them rightly, the law in its ordaining of what is good is not burdensome."

[167]On the hierarchy of the angels, see Part II, note 32, infra.

[168]Consequently, in the phrasing of the issue as formulated at the beginning of the first question, Aquinas is adopting the view that civil power is "a natural institution" and not simply a "punishment of a corrupt nature." (See note 162, supra.)

> The mode of sovereignty is two-fold, one ordained for guiding, the other, however, for dominating. Thus, the sovereignty of the master in relation to the slave is, as the Philosopher says, that of the absolute ruler to the subject. However, the absolute ruler differs from the king, as the Philosopher says in the same place, because the king arranges his sovereignty for the good of the nation over which he presides, promulgating statutes and laws because of their usefulness to the nation.[169]

Aquinas accepts the fact that the "dominating" mode of sovereignty is coercive only and would not have existed in the state of innocence. Nevertheless, the "guiding" mode responds to a need of the human being, considered as rational, which would require attention regardless of the state of human existence. Simply put, even man in the most rational of environments has an inherent need for complementarity and guidance. He writes:

> The first sovereignty, which was established for the advantage of the subjects, did exist then [i.e., before sin] with respect to some needs though not for all. . . . But so far as the first need only, namely, that which is for guidance in action or in knowledge, it follows that one greater than another was

---

[169]II Scriptum super Libros Sent. 44,1,3, Solutio. The references to Aristotle appear to be to the Nicomachean Ethics, Book 8, Chapter 10, particularly $1160^b 26$-30 (comparison of master/slave and tyrant/subjects) and $1160^b 1$-8 (contrast of king and tyrant). On the comparison of the relation of master/slave and tyrant/subjects, see also the Politics, Book 1, Chapter 3, $1253^b 15$-23. Aristotle's controversial discussion of slavery as a natural institution appears in the two chapters of the Politics which follow this passage.

endowed with the employment of wisdom and with the light of the intellect.[170]

In responding to the enumerated arguments favoring the conventional view, Aquinas insists that the notion of a state of innocence need not be viewed as excluding the need for guidance. Civil authority always has at least a minimum, essential value for man. He accepts the dictum of Gregory, to the effect that all men are by nature free, but with a qualification. They are "equal in freedom, but not in natural perfections."[171] Aquinas' "guiding" mode of sovereignty does not prejudice this qualified natural freedom.

Having made this distinction between the "guiding" and "dominating" modes of sovereignty, Aquinas is in a position to turn aside arguments which rely upon Augustine and St. Paul, without explicitly repudiating their views. Their arguments can be accepted and absorbed, for they only pertain to the second mode.[172]

In the first question, therefore, Aquinas has established that there is some minimum positive value to civil authority. He has also removed the problem of civil authority from direct involvement in the theological problem of evil, except as to the purely coercive mode. In particularly egregious cases, this mode is still to be explained in terms of the conventional view of civil authority. In the second question, Aquinas turns to more technical issues concerning the obedience which is rightly due to sovereigns. He begins with a preliminary question in the first article, namely, whether obedience itself is a virtue at all.[173] It should

---

[170]II Scriptum super Libros Sent. 44,1,3, Solutio.

[171]Ibid., 44,1,3, ad 1.

[172]Ibid., 44,1,3, ad 2-4.

[173]This issue is taken up again by Aquinas in the Summa Theologiae. See ST, II-II, Q. 104, a.

be noted, however, that in the present article, as in the preceding one, Aristotle figures as an <u>auctoritas</u> on both sides of the argument.

For example, in support of the argument that obedience is not itself a virtue, the first enumerated argument cites Aristotle's technical definition that a virtue is the means of two vices.[174] How can obedience be of this sort, the argument proceeds, since one cannot err in an overabundance of obedience? Similarly, one argument notes that obedience is neither a cardinal virtue (of which there are only four) nor a collateral virtue, "as is clear if the collateral virtues are considered to be those which the Philosopher enumerates."[175]

---

2. The discussion of obedience in the <u>Summa</u> is of importance as a parallel to much of the discussion in the second question of Distinction 44 in the sentential commentary.

[174] II <u>Scriptum super Libros Sent.</u> 44,2,1,1. The Aristotelian text referenced is the <u>Nicomachean Ethics</u>, Book 2, Chapter 6, and particularly 1106^b35-1107^a1-3: "Virtue, then, is a state of character concerned with choice, lying in a mean, i.e. the mean relative to us, this being determined by a rational principle, and by that principle by which the man of practical wisdom would determine it. Now it is a mean between two vices, that which depends on excess and that which depends on effect. . . ."

[175] II <u>Scriptum super Libros Sent.</u> 44,2,1,3. The reference is to the <u>Nicomachean Ethics</u>, Book 4, passim. See also II <u>Scriptum super Libros Sent.</u> 44,2,1,5, arguing from Aristotle's discussion of legal justice in the <u>Nicomachean Ethics</u>, Book 5, Chapter 1, and particularly 1129^b12-15, 25-28: "Since the lawless man was seen to be unjust and the law-abiding man just, evidently all lawful acts are in a sense just acts; for the acts laid down by the legislative art are lawful, and each of these . . . is just. . . . This form of justice, then, is complete virtue, but not absolutely, but in relation to our neighbor. And therefore justice is often thought to be the greatest of virtues . . . and proverbially 'in justice is every virtue

In response, Aquinas' <u>Solutio</u> takes the position that obedience is a particular virtue.[176] Much of this argument relies upon the use of the <u>Nicomachean Ethics</u> as authority for this position.[177] Obedience may seem general, in the sense that it is the object of action directed towards any of the virtues. Yet, just as Aristotle points out in the case of a concept like "magnanimity,"[178] Aquinas argues, we may say that

---

comprehended'." The status of justice is therefore problematic within the Aristotelian system.

[176]II <u>Scriptum super Libros Sent.</u> 44,2,1, <u>Solutio</u>. Thus, the <u>Solutio</u> seeks to resolve a problem which in fact arises within the Aristotelian system. (Cf. note 175, supra, discussing the sense in which legal justice is coincident with virtue.) This problem is addressed by Aristotle with respect to the status of justice as a virtue in the <u>Nicomachean Ethics</u>, Book 5, Chapters 1 and 2, passim. Hence the argumentation in this article, both in the enumerated arguments and the opposing <u>Solutio</u>, represents a reworking of this problem with respect to the status of obedience. What is exhibited by the article taken as a whole, therefore, is the project of assimilation of Aristotelian principles at a fairly developed and subtle level. Both sides of the argument begin from Aristotelian premises, and in the aggregate only can they be said to convey the Aristotelian position represented in the <u>Ethics</u>.

[177]See Part II, text at notes 46-49, infra.

[178]There is some problem in determining the antecedents of this text. The Mandonnet edition of the <u>Scriptum super Libros Sent.</u> gives the <u>Nicomachean Ethics</u>, Book 4, Chapter 8 as the reference. In fact, this chapter concerns the virtue of "ready-wittedness," which also includes within it the virtue of tact or tastefulness. However, the authority is cited to illustrate, by analogy, how a virtue may be specific (and have a specific object), while at the same time, in a different sense, it may be general since it is discovered in many different circumstances. That

obedience is a specific virtue with a specific object, that of "harmonizing command with obligation,"[179] even though this virtue is seen as part of the general matter of all virtues.[180]

Furthermore, responding to a technical objection with respect to the principles of Aristotelian ethics, Aquinas argues that obedience is indeed a mean between two vices. There can be an overabundance of obedience (an overabundance being one end of the poles of vice), "not related to an excess in terms of quantity ('how much'), . . . but . . . in terms of its essence ('what')."[181] That is to say, one may be overabundant in obedience when one obeys uncritically in "what" one ought not to obey.

It is the second article of this question which returns to an issue of specific importance to the analysis of civil authority, namely, whether Christians are required to obey secular authorities. Aquinas is well aware that, on the issue of this specific duty of obedience, the critical question involves the appropriate response of the Christian to the tyrant, or absolute ruler.[182] Here the mode

---

being the nature of the argument, reference to Book 4, Chapter 8 does not seem particularly apposite. It may be that a better reference would be to Book 4, Chapter 2, concerning "magnificence," since this virtue will be manifested in a wide variety of circumstances and can be determined only by its appropriateness in the circumstances. (See, e.g., 1123a10-18, passim: ". . . but what is magnificent here is what is magnificent in these circumstances. . . .") The most striking parallel for purposes of Aquinas' discussion of the status of obedience as a virtue remains, however, Aristotle's discussion of the status of justice. (Cf., e.g., notes 175-176, supra.)

[179]II Scriptum super Libros Sent. 44,2,1, Solutio.

[180]Cf., ibid., ad 2, 5 and 6.

[181]Ibid., ad 1.

[182]Hence the emphasis in the statement of the

66

of sovereignty, already determined by Aquinas to be of inherent positive value,[183] is exercised in a questionable manner.

The article opens with a series of enumerated arguments for the proposition that Christians are not required to obey secular authorities at all. The argumentation presents an extreme version of the conventional view of civil authority. If the acceptance of Christianity "frees" the believer, then he should no longer be subject to the strictures of obedience to any earthly sovereign.[184] Subjection is, after all, a condition of the corrupt state of man, and acceptance of the faith should free him from such subjection.[184]

Beyond this general attitude towards civil authority, the problem of a subject's relation to a tyrant is thought to support this extreme proposition. If the tyrant has usurped his position, then it is appropriate that "as the power for rebelling against them is conceded, men are not required to obey."[186]

It would appear, therefore, that the enumerated arguments taken as a whole represent an extreme form of the conventional view. In fact, it may be argued, the position taken by these arguments is too extreme; it is this attitude of radical separation of the believer from political experience and political obligation which the conventional view itself seeks to moderate. The theodicy of the conventional view can be seen to justify the

---

issue raised by the second article, *et maxime tyrannis*.

[183]See II *Scriptum super Libros Sent.* 44,1,2, Solutio.

[184]*Ibid.*, 44,2,2,1.

[185]*Ibid.*, 44,2,2,2. Cf. *ibid.*, 44,2,2,3.

[186]*Ibid.*, 44,2,2,4. Specific support is claimed from Cicero's justification of the assasination of Caesar. See *ibid.*, 44,2,5, citing Cicero's *De officiis* 1:26.

continuation of political obligation to the "freed" believer.[187] Furthermore, one need not endorse the conventional view at all to accept at least the apparent force of the arguments concerning tyrants. The duty owed to a tyrant is problematic under any view of political obligation.[188]

The extreme nature of the position notwithstanding, the notion that the "liberation" of the sinner upon acceptance of the faith may be given subversive connotations. The conventional view cures this only by devaluing civil authority and characterizing it as an instrument of divine punishment. It responds to the dilemma created by a theology of liberation which had to survive within an often actively hostile political environment.[189]

The *Sed contra* takes an opposite but equally extreme position. It relies upon the words of Peter, who, faced no doubt with the dilemma mentioned above, urges his readers to "be submissive to [their] masters. . . ."[190] The *Sed contra* also refers to Romans 13:2, part of the Scriptural *locus*

---

[187]On the nature of the conventional view as a justification of political obligation, see John B. Morrall, *Political Thought in Medieval Times* (New York: Harper Torchbooks, 1962), pp. 28 *et seq.* and 68 *et seq.*

[188]Cicero's justification of the assasins of Caesar, cited in II *Scriptum super Libros Sent.* 44,2,2,5, can hardly be viewed in itself as an example of the Patristic, conventional view of civil authority.

[189]See generally W. T. Jones, *A History of Western Philosophy*. 2nd ed., Vol. II: *The Medieval Mind* (New York: Harcourt Brace Jovanovich, Inc., 1969), pp. 21-31, passim: "[T]he Christians seemed a menace to the unity and solidarity of the state. . . ."

[190]I Peter 2:18, quoted in II *Scriptum super Libros Sent.* 44,2,2, *Sed contra*. See Part II, note 54, infra.

classicus of the problem of civil authority,[191] in which Paul asserts, "he who resists authority, resists the ordinance of God." From this assertion, the Sed contra infers that no resistence to civil authority is permissible.

Aquinas' Solutio follows from his previous discussion of the inherent positive value of civil authority.[192] Inherent to sovereignty, that is, in its mode or form, there is order, and the authority responds to man's natural need for guidance. The obedience due to the sovereign will depend upon the appropriateness of the command. The obligation, in our present (corrupted) state, arises in a two-fold manner, both from the coercive mode and the inherent orderliness of the relation of sovereign/subject. In discussing these bases of obligation, Aquinas' analysis also depends upon his previous examination of the source of civil authority.[193] On the present question he states:

> this duty is caused by the order of a sovereignty which possesses a constraining force, not only temporally but also spiritually as a matter of conscience, as the Apostle says, insofar as the order of sover-eignty derives from God. . . .[194]

Accordingly, at least to the extent that sovereignty does derive from God, it possesses inherently the mode of orderliness which impels the obligation of obedience on the part of the subject. Implicitly, Aquinas has already rejected the more general version of the extreme position taken in the

---

[191]Cf. A.P. d'Entreves, The Medieval Contribution to Political Thought, p. 7.

[192]See II Scriptum super Libros Sent. 44,1,3, Solutio.

[193]See ibid., 44,1,2, Solutio.

[194]Ibid., 44,2,2, Solutio. The reference to "the Apostle" (i.e., St. Paul) is probably to Romans 13:3-6. See Part II, note 57, infra.

enumerated arguments of the article.[195] For if the obligation to obey is inherent because the mode of sovereignty is derived from God, then the acceptance of faith on the part of the believer can hardly be expected to negate that obligation.

To what extent, then, might sovereignty be said not to derive from God? It may be argued that Aquinas' analysis of this questions parallels his treatment of the problem of the source of the potential for sin.[196] That is to say, in principle the mode of sovereignty (orderliness, the right to coerce and to guide) derives from God, but the activation of this principle may involve a deviation deriving from the human actor. Aquinas notes two distinct situations which may involve deviation from the mode or form of sovereignty, either the manner in which it is acquired or the manner in which it is utilized. It should be noted that Aquinas now appears to be addressing the two enumerated arguments specifically directed to the problem of the duty owed to the tyrant.[197] To a certain extent, he accepts the reasoning of these arguments, although he establishes the essential mode or form of sovereignty, its inherent positive value, as the basis for deciding the question. In this regard he writes:

> sovereignty can fail to be from God in two ways: either as to the mode of acquiring sovereignty, or as to the abuse of sovereignty. As to the first, it happens in two ways: either because of a defect of the person . . . or because of a defect in the mode of acquisition itself. . . . From the first defect, he is not impeded from acquiring the right of sovereignty, and since sovereignty with respect to its form is always from God, . . . this creates the duty of obedience. . . . But . . . he who

---

[195]See ibid., 44,2,2,1-3.

[196]See ibid., 44,1,1, Solutio.

[197]See ibid., 44,2,2, 4-5.

usurps civil power through violence does not truly become a sovereign or master.[198]

The principal defect of this activation of the potential for authority lies in the disorder inherent in usurpation. If the essential positive value of civil authority is the orderliness it imposes upon the human community, either through its "commanding" or through its "guiding" mode, then the disorder which is implied in subversion by a usurper is critical.[199]

The second way in which the activation of this potential may be defective concerns its abusive exercise. This situation is not addressed by the enumerated arguments, and yet it may be the more significant issue for political theory. The question concerns the limits of civil authority. From the perspective of the subject, the question may be characterized as one concerning the

---

[198]Ibid., 44,2,2, Solutio. Thus, Aquinas affirms the position taken by the last two enumerated arguments, saying that "those who attain authority through violence are not true rulers." Ibid., 44,2,2, ad 4. Similarly, he accepts Cicero's justification of the assasins of Caesar, but with qualifications: such an assasination is justified if "the subjects [are] unwilling or even forced to consent, and . . . there is no recourse to a superior authority. . . ." Ibid., 44,2,2, ad 5. (On the significance of these qualifications, see note 199, infra.) Particularly in light of the second qualification, therefore, one may argue that Aquinas would insist upon an inherent right of subjects to petition a higher civil authority in any political system consisting of a hierarchy of delegated authority.

[199]Correspondingly, the disorder created by usurpation can be cured by the reassertion of order, even though the usurper retains the office of civil authority attained improperly. His civil authority is secure in principle if "afterwards he becomes a true master, either through the consent of the subjects or through the authority of superiors." Ibid., 44,2,2, Solutio.

appropriate and permissible response of the subject to abuse of power, even assuming <u>arguendo</u> that the power was rightfully possessed by the abuser in the first place. In this context, Aquinas raises the issue of the right, or even the duty, to deny the authority of the sovereign. He writes:

> [T]here can be an abuse of authority in two ways. Either . . . what is commanded by a sovereign is contrary to that for which the sovereignty is established, as if it commands an act of sin contrary to virtue, for the protection and preservation of which the sovereignty is established. In that case, one is not only not required to obey, one is even required not to obey. . . . Or. . . he compels that to which the order of sovereignty does not extend itself. . . . In that case, the subject is not required to obey, nor indeed is he required not to obey.[200]

In the second case, the abuse of sovereign authority is relative to specific, positive strictures on the scope of the sovereign's authority. Here, the resulting disorder does not go to the very heart of the notion of order in the relation between sovereign and subject. Presumably, the remedy for this sort of abuse would be internal to the system of positive rules which are operative within the community.

Since civil authority is essentially directed to the establishment of order in the human community, it should not be viewed as inimical to the "liberation" of the believer in acceptance of his faith. Hence, civil authority "is established for the benefit of the subjects [and] does not abolish the freedom of the subjects."[201] Nevertheness, one

---

[200]<u>Ibid</u>.

[201]<u>Ibid</u>., 44,2,2, ad 1. Alternatively, however, Aquinas speculates that, when Christ is reported to say that "the children are free," he was referring only to himself and the disciples. In

Nevertheless, one still finds some ambiguity in Aquinas' text on the issue of whether the conventional view *per se* should be rejected. In responding to the argument that baptism has the effect of liberating the believer of all disabilities arising from the dissolution of the state of pure innocence, he argues that the penalties of the servile condition are not thereby eliminated, "though that [condition] is a punishment for sin."[202]

In the third article of the second question, Aquinas raises the highly specialized issue of the duty of obedience which members of religious orders owe to their prelate. It may seem out of place to have such a discussion inserted into an analysis of civil authority, and yet it must be kept in mind that the question of authority within the highly developed hierarchical structure of the church was undoubtedly a topical issue. Nor should we forget that the question of the relative duties owed by *magistri* who were members of religious communities was involved in the controversy between the orders and the university authorities. This controversy

---

that case "only those who follow the apostolic life" would be free from the duty to obey civil authorities. (*Ibid.*) This speculation therefore continues the tension between the relative authority of *rex* and *sacerdos*, leaving open the possibility that the civil power cannot exercise any authority over clerics. On the medieval controversy over the competence of civil and ecclesiastical sovereigns, see R.W. & A.J. Carlyle, *A History of Mediaeval Political Theory in the West*, Vol. IV: *The Theories of the Relation of the Empire and the Papacy from the Tenth Century to the Twelfth* (London: W. Blackwood and Sons, 1932), ch. IV, passim.

[202] II *Scriptum super Libros Sent.* 44,2,2, ad 2. It may be with this argument in mind that Aquinas argues that "the bond by which one is bound in baptism is compatible with the bond of servitude." (*Ibid.*, ad 3.) Hence, to some extent the conventional view of authority is retained, despite Aquinas' position in *ibid.*, 44,1,3, *Solutio*, which at least in part appears to reject that view.

kept both Aquinas and Bonaventure from being received by the University of Paris until the pope intervened on their behalf.[203]

Moreover, aside from its topicality, the issue raised by the third article does offer a more specialized case of the notion of "authority" against which to test its meaning. This may be seen to have results even for our own understanding of the more general case, that of the duties of the subject to civil authority.[204] The discussion here is, nevertheless, somewhat specialized, and it will have only an indirect applicability to the analysis of the problem of civil authority.

Aquinas places this discussion in juxtaposition to the analysis of the duty of obedience owed to sovereigns in the second article. That juxtaposition appears to be intentional on the author's part. Some of the discussion in the present article elaborates upon the earlier one. In particular, we have seen Aquinas argue that, in cases where the sovereign oversteps the bounds of his authority, the duty of the subject may be negated. How, then, are such cases to be recognized, and by whom? This issue is pursued incidentally in the course of the third article.

The enumerated arguments which open the discussion take the position that members of religious orders are required to obey their prelates in all things. Part of this position involves the following argument:

> [J]udgment concerning a superior is not left to an inferior. But if the subject had to determine in which matters he was to obey and in which

---

[203]See E. Gilson, The Philosophy of St. Bonaventure trans. I. Trethowan and F. J. Sheed (New York: Sheed & Ward, 1940), pp. 10-14.

[204]Since the subject also has a duty of obedience to the prelate, this article may even relate directly to our understanding of the subject's general duties. Cf. II Scriptum super Libros Sent. 44,2,3,4-5, ad 4-5.

not, judgment concerning the command of the superior would be left to the subject himself.205

In his Solutio, here as elsewhere in his commentary on this distinction, Aquinas emphasizes that the authority under question is intended as a means of promoting orderliness in the community, here one governed by a set of explicit rules (Regula).206 Hence, the obedience due to the religious authority, the prelate, is limited to those rules and the purposes which those rules are intended to serve. Accordingly, it is for the subject to decide in his own mind when a command exceeds the scope of the duty of obedience.207

The third major division of the commentary is the Literal Exposition, which is for the most part no more than a critique of Lombard's texts.208 An exception to this characterization is the curious passage, appearing at the end of the commentary,209 which, in the form of an articulus, addresses the question of whether a greater power is to be obeyed to a greater extent than a lesser power.210 Whether

---

205Ibid., 44,2,3,4.

206See ibid., 44,2,3, Solutio: "[A]uthorities are established in religious orders so the condition of the order is preserved according to precepts of the rule. [O]nly in what pertains to a rule is the duty of obedience created."

207Ibid., ad 4: "[A]lthough the subject is not to judge the command of the prelate, . . . he is to judge concerning the particular act to the extent to which he is not subject to the prelate. . . . [I]t does not follow that he is to obey in all things; to the contrary, it is necessary that he not obey in certain things."

208Cf. text at notes 103-108, supra.

209See Part II, text at notes 75-82, infra.

210Cf. note 121, supra. The passage is formally elliptical, however, lacking a Sed contra; nor does it identify the Solutio as such. Mandonnet suggests that the passage may nevertheless be read

or not this is merely an extraneous interpolation in the redaction of Aquinas' sentential commentary,[211] it does complete the discussion begun earlier in the second article of the second question, in which Aquinas qualifies the right to rebel against a tyrant if such a usurper "becomes a true master . . . through the authority of superiors."[212] What, then, is the orderly relationship among civil authorities within one civil hierarchy? The question follows naturally from Aquinas' earlier discussion, and it is also suggested by Lombard's text,[213] which argues, quoting Augustine, that a countermanding command of a higher civil authority (e.g., the proconsul) would cancel one's duty to obey the command of an inferior civil authority (e.g., the procurator). Hence, there is a need to identify the relationship among these related superior and inferior civil authorities.

Having raised this issue in his Literal Exposition, Aquinas sets forth a series of four enumerated arguments for the proposition that a greater power is not necessarily to be obeyed to a greater extent. The arguments are based upon a recognition that the specific competence of any authority, strictly as to matters within its competence, is exclusive to the authority possessing that competence. So, for example, relying upon Aristotle's *Nicomachean Ethics*, Aquinas argues that the paterfamilias may be a "lesser" authority than the general of the army in the abstract, but in certain matters the one will have exclusive competence, and in certain others, the other.[214] The

---

as an article. See Part II, note 76, infra.

[211]Mandonnet seems to believe that the passage is authentic, if oddly placed. See Part II, note 76, infra.

[212]II *Scriptum super Libros Sent.* 44,2,2, Solutio and ad 5. See also note 199 and accompanying text, supra.

[213]See Part I, text at notes 18-20, infra.

[214]II *Scriptum super Libros Sent.* 44, Expositio 1. The reference is to the *Nicomachean Ethics*, Book 9, Chapter 2, passim. E.g., 1165^a14-17, 25-27: "That

arguments point out similar divisions of competence among ecclesiastical authorities,[215] and finally raise the problem of rex and sacerdos:

> [T]he spiritual authority is higher than the secular. Thus, if the greater authority is to be obeyed to a greater extent, then the spiritual prelate will always be able to absolve us from a command of the secular authority, which is false.[216]

To resolve this issue, Aquinas identifies an ambiguity in the notion of "superior" and "inferior" authority. In one sense, one authority is "inferior" to another because it proceeds entirely from it. In this sense the latter is always to be preferred over the former. The authority of God is the clear example of this for Aquinas, and rex and sacerdos are so by analogy, each within its own competence:

> [T]he authority of God is thus for every created authority, the authority of the emperor for the authority of the proconsul, the authority of the pope for every spiritual authority in the Church.[217]

In a second sense, "superior" and "inferior" authorities might both be ranked under a common

---

we should not make the same return to everyone . . . is plain enough; . . . we ought to render to each class what is appropriate and becoming. . . . [F]or that matter one should not give the same honour to one's father and one's mother, nor again should one give them the honour due to a philosopher or to a general, but the honour due to a father, or again to a mother."

[215] II Scriptum super Libros Sent. 44, Expositio, 2-3.

[216] Ibid., 44, Expositio, 4.

[217] Ibid., Respondeo.

source. In that sense their relationship one to the other depends upon the directive of the higher authority which they have in common. Aquinas writes:

> [T]he superior and the inferior authority can be such that both proceed from one particular supreme authority which subjects one to the other as it wills, and then the one is not superior to the other except in what the one is subordinated to the other by the supreme authority. In these things only is the superior to be obeyed to a greater extent than the inferior.[218]

Under this interpretation, the arguments concerning the conflicting authority of father and general, or between the various authorities within the ecclesiastical hierarchy are all examples of correlative authorities, all of which are ultimately subject to some other supreme source of authority.[219]

On the delicate question raised by the fourth enumerated argument, namely, the relationship between emperor and pope, Aquinas likewise tries to treat these two authorities as correlative, each having its own competence, as authorized by God.[220]

---

[218]Ibid.

[219]Ibid., ad 1-3.

[220]It is Gilson's view that for Aquinas the relation between pope and emperor is one of subordination, not correlation, the later in fact being Dante's Averroistic gloss. (See, e.g., E. Gilson, *Dante the Philosopher*, trans. David Moore (New York: Sheed & Ward, 1949).) To the contrary, Carlyle accepts the correlative view, with perhaps a degree of indirect influence over secular matters available in addition to the spiritual sovereign. (See R. W. & A. J. Carlyle, *A History of Mediaeval Political Theory in the West*, vol. V: *The Political Theory of the Thirteenth Century* (London: W. Blackwood and Sons, 1938), pp. 353-4: "[W]hile in

To that extent, each is "superior," but neither is superior in the absolute sense. He adds, however, the following cryptic qualification, with which the commentary is brought abruptly to an end:

> Unless, perhaps, the secular authority is conjoined to the spiritual authority, as in the pope, who holds the crown of each authority, spiritual and secular. . . .[221]

This sudden assertion of primacy on behalf of the pope does not seem warranted from the discussion that precedes it. Of course, there may be a degree of technical accuracy to this position, since, within his temporal domains at least, the pope did exercise both spiritual and temporal authority. This narrow, technical reading of the passage does not, however, seem to account adequately for its apparent connotation, namely, that the overall discussion at this point concerns the pope and the emperor. This suggestion would seem, therefore, to be contrary both to the discussion in this part of the Literal Exposition, as well as to the discussion of the second article of the first question, arguing that civil authority has its source in God.

It is difficult to know what weight Aquinas intended to give to this cryptic qualification. Whether or not it is significant that the discussion is tacked onto the end of the Literal Exposition, rather than being placed in the body of the commentary, it is at least noteworthy that the passage is introduced by the formulaic phrase, "unless, perhaps" (<u>nisi forte</u>). It is known that this phrase is sometimes used by Aquinas

---

the one passage [in the sentential commentary], he [Aquinas] claims for the Pope the supreme power both in temporal and spiritual matters, his treatment of the subject both in the 'Summa Theologica' and in the 'De Regimine Principum' suggests that his normal and mature judgment was that the Pope had an indirect rather than a direct authority in temporal matters.")

[221]<u>Ibid</u>., ad 4.

ironically.[222] We may therefore question how seriously we must take into account the discussion that follows that introductory phrase, particularly since that brief discussion is so manifestly at odds with the discussion that precedes it.

Summary of the Features of the Sentential Commentary

In this commentary we have found Aquinas freely departing from the structure and content of the text of Lombard. In particular, the discussion in the commentary is more decidedly interested in the question of the nature and limits of authority, and especially of civil authority.

In the service of this commentary, Aquinas shows himself skilled in the use of <u>auctoritates</u>.[223]

---

[222] See Part II, note 81, infra. That the <u>nisi forte</u> clause is to be read as limiting the scope of any discussion which follows it is now well understood. "[I]n religious matters [Aquinas] declared that the ecclesiatical power is to be obeyed rather than the civil, and in civil matters the lay power is to be obeyed rather than the ecclesiastical, except perhaps (<u>nisi forte</u>) in the special case of the two powers' being amalgamated in one person, such as the Roman pontiff. Commentators discussing this last example, and not armed with a realization of the significance of its exceptive (<u>nisi forte</u>) structure, have inferred from it that Aquinas here committed himself to an extreme papalist position which would endow the pope with the fulness of spiritual and temporal power. However, once the significance of that structure has been gathered from the many other available textual examples, the conclusion may be drawn that Aquinas taught the separation of these powers as a matter of principle, yet he also observed the local fact that insofar as the pope is a temporal ruler of papal territory, he, exceptionally, holds both spiritual and temporal power." <u>The Encyclopedia of Philosophy</u>, 1972 Reprint ed., s.v. "Medieval Philosophy," by Desmond Paul Henry.

[223] For an excellent study of Aquinas' facility in the use Platonic <u>auctoritates</u>, see R. J. Henle,

Even at this early stage, Aristotle figures in the discussion, but it would be inaccurate to say that the text is solely, or even primarily, concerned with the task of assimilating Aristotle into Christian philosophy.

Does the sentential commentary, as represented by the portion considered in this analysis, appear to represent the critical choices in principles and method in Aquinas' philosophy? While a full answer to this question must await the comparative analysis of Aquinas' later efforts, to be undertaken in the next section, it certainly seems likely that one can find these choices in the sentential commentary. Clearly, the style of analysis, made classic in the Summa, is fully evident in the sentential commentary. In terms of choice of basic principles, the situation is less clear.

We have seen previously that Aquinas has already introduced Aristotle into his thought as an auctoritas. However, as may be clear in the discussion of Bonaventure to be undertaken later, Aquinas is not alone in referring to Aristotle. Further, on its own merits, Aquinas' sentential commentary remains somewhat tentative in its resolution of various issues, notably the question of whether or not to replace the conventional view of civil authority with the natural view.

Accordingly, it does not seem warranted to assert, with Mondin, that the sentential commentary represents the highest example of Aquinas' speculative rigor and originality. Final judgment on this score must nevertheless await the comparative analysis of parallel passages in the more mature work of Aquinas.

This much may be said about the basic features of Aquinas' sentential commentary on the problem of civil authority. First, the rigorous argumentation that would be employed in later works, developed within the well-defined framework of the quaestio and articulus, is already evident in the commentary. Second, there is a strong indication that Aquinas is drawing away decisively from the purely conventional

---

Saint Thomas and Platonism (The Hague: Martinus Nijhoff, 1970).

view of civil authority, though on some specific issues he may seem ambiguous. Third, Aristotle is already a signficant inspiration in much of the argumentation encountered within the commentary, although it would be perhaps an exaggeration to say that the text of the commentary is distinctly Aristotelian. Fourth, and related to the preceding point, to the extent that a project of assimilation of Aristotelianism is already under way in this early work, it does not follow that this project entails the jettisoning of other philosophical traditions. Augustine and thinkers avowedly following in his tradition remain important sources of authority throughout the commentary.

On the merits of his original thought as expressed in the commentary, the following remarks may be made. Aquinas appears to take the position that our capacity for moral action does arise from God; that is to say, it is a moral capacity within man and natural to him. Evil and suffering in the world are a result of human choices deviating from the moral norm, and man carries the responsibility for these actions. While civil authority as an institution may have a coercive element to it in our present circumstances, it has an essentially positive value and is likewise natural to man. It is a valid, justifiable, human institution, finding its validity, in Aquinas' view, in its divine source. Since it is a moral institution, serving an essentially positive function which is natural to man, men have a natural obligation to obey civil authorities.

Having located the source of this natural human institution in God, Aquinas rejects any radical millenial view that would claim that the acceptance of a religious bond negates the natural obligation of obedience to civil authority. In the case of the sovereignty of a tyrant, of course, particularly acute moral problems arise for the subject. Again relying upon the essential positive value of civil authority in principle, Aquinas sets the norm of obedience as the basis of relationship between sovereign and subject, even where sovereignty is achieved unworthily.

However, where the usurper has utilized violence to attain the position of sovereignty, this in itself negates the orderliness that underlies the concept of civil authority. The duty to obey such a sovereign may therefore be lifted, although not under all circumstances. In the worst cases of abuse of authority, however, the citizen or subject has not only the right, but the explicit duty to reject the authority of the tyrant.

It remains to be seen the extent to which Aquinas elaborates upon this approach to the problem of civil authority in his mature philosophical efforts. We must also examine whether he is able to resolve some of the ambiguities encountered in his sentential commentary. This is especially so as to the status of the conventional view of civil authority which had been so much a part of the heritage of medieval political philosophy.

IV. AQUINAS' LATER WRITINGS

Textual Analysis

In examining the later writings of Aquinas on the problem of civil authority, two issues in particular come to the fore: (i) the essentially natural condition of authority; and, (ii) the extent of the obedience owed to civil authorities, including tyrants. In addition, in the later writings the problem of civil authority begins to emerge as a discrete philosophical issue, not simply an outgrowth of the problem of the potential for evil. In large degree, this emergence may be a result of the fact that Aquinas is not constrained by the structure nominally imposed by Lombard's Sentences.

However, we can find "no 'politics' of St. Thomas Aquinas. This is certainly true in the sense that he has left us no complete work to which we can turn . . . for a systematic treatment of politics."[224] In comparison with the context of the sentential commentary, however, Aquinas' later writings do provide us with identifiable and extended treatments of issues of political and legal philo-

---

[224]A. P. d'Entreves, Introduction to Selected Politial Writings, by Thomas Aquinas (Oxford: Basil Blackwell, 1948), p. viii.

sophy, including the problem of civil authority. This noticeable concentration of issues around their own center of gravity is itself a significant development from the point of view of textual analysis.

Some of the sources in Aquinas' later writings are problematic. Two opuscula in particular, the De regimine principum and the De regimine Judaeorum, would at first glance seem to be pertinent to the present study. Yet the latter, a reply to an inquiry from the Duchess of Brabant, is directed to the very specific question of the propriety of exacting tribute from Jewish subjects under the jurisdiction of a Christian sovereign.[225] It has little or no bearing upon the present inquiry.

The former work is indeed of interest to the present inquiry, but there are textual problems in characterizing it as a systematic treatment of Aquinas. As has been noted by d'Entreves,

> The treatise De Regimine Principum is of little avail for the purpose. Only the first book and a small part of the second can be attributed with certainty to St. Thomas' authoriship. They cover a limited ground and cannot be considered exhaustive.[226]

As we shall see, this opusculum does contain some analysis that will be of use in tracking the development of Aquinas' thought on the specific issue of the nature and extent of civil authority. However, there is another limitation on the utility of this work for purposes of the present analysis; the work is a political tract with a preordained audience, namely, the King of Cyprus. Possibly in consequence of this fact, the text of the opusculum is cautious, diplomatic and hortatory.

Throughout the period 1265-1273,[227] Aquinas had prepared a series of commentaries on various

---

[225]See Selected Political Writings, pp. 84-95.

[226]A. P. d'Entreves, p. viii.

[227]See The Encyclopedia of Philosophy, 1972 Reprint ed., s.v. "Thomas Aquinas, St.," by Vernon

treatises of Aristotle, including the Nicomachean Ethics and the Politics.228 One might therefore hope to find a "systematic treatment of politics" in his commentaries on these two works. Unfortunately, this hope would be misplaced. As d'Entreves has emphasized,

> The Commentaries on the Ethics and the Politics of Aristotle are a valuable source of information. But apart from the doubts as to the authenticity of some of their parts, the Scholastic form of expounding the Aristotelian text makes it difficult to distinguish St. Thomas' own views from those which he attributed to his author.229

Chenu's comments on this issue are perhaps more instructive. It is by no means impossible to ascertain with whose voice the commentator is speaking. "The medieval commentator implicitly makes the contents of the text his own, and if he does not accept it, he says so explicitly whereas he is presumed to make it his own, if he says nothing."230 Nevertheless, one must admit that it is not in the

---

J. Bourke. Chenu gives the dates 1261-1272. See M.-D. Chenu, Toward Understanding Saint Thomas trans. A.-M. Landry and D. Hughes (Chicago: Henry Regnery Company, 1964), p. 205.

228In X Libros Ethicorum. (Available in English as Commentary on the Nicomachean Ethics, 2 vols. trans. C.I. Litzinger (Chicago: Henry Regnery Company, 1964).) In Libros Politicorum. (Translation of Book III, Lectures 1-6 by E. L. Fortin and P.D. O'Neill available in R. Lerner and M. Mahdi, eds. Medieval Political Philosophy (Ithaca, N.Y.: Cornell University Press, 1978), pp. 297-334. The commentary on the Politics was left unfinished by Aquinas at Book III, Chapter 8, and was completed by Peter of Auvergne, his pupil after 1268. See Chenu, p. 224.

229A. P. d'Entreves, p. viii.

230Chenu, pp. 207-8. Lerner and Mahdi would go further in citing the Aristotelian commentaries as

Aristotelian commentaries that one can find Aquinas' own systematic choices in philosophical doctrine. In general agreement with the basic view expressed by d'Entreves, Chenu cautions:

> Let us place concern for literal meaning as topmost in the intentions of Saint Thomas [in his Aristotelian commentaries]. . . . Counter to the paraphrastic procedure employed by Albert, Saint Thomas was . . . thoroughly preoccupied with the literal sense and committed himself to an exegesis of the text.[231]

Hence, in seeking Aquinas' own philosophical choices on the problem of civil authority, one cannot focus on the Aristotelian commentaries without skewing the analysis to a significant degree. In these commentaries, "Saint Thomas brings his whole effort to bear upon a minute and closely literal analysis. Tradition supplied him with two types of interpretation: the paraphrase and the piecemeal literal commentary. . . . [C]ircumstances . . . moved him to make use of the second method. . . ."[232] Ironically, the sentential commentary,

---

sources of Aquinas' political teachings. "Aquinas' teachings on political philosophy are to be found especially in his commentaries on the Ethics and the Politics, in his short treatise [De regimine principum], and in various articles of his Summa Theologiae." Lerner and Mahdi, p. 273. How-ever, even they admit the essentially literal character of the Aristotelian commentary. "It is characterized . . . by its literalness . . . and by the extreme care with which it scrutinizes the text." Ibid. On the whole, Chenu's opinion in this matter is to be preferred. "It would be to falsify, however, . . . the correct equilibrium of [the Aristotelian commentary] -- and, therefore, the intention of Saint Thomas -- to seek in the commentaries his personal thought and to build a Thomism whose . . . philosophy [would be] in his commentaries on Aristotle." Chenu, p. 214.

[231]Chenu, p. 208.

[232]Ibid., p. 220.

bound by no literal strictures, may prove to have been a more useful source of Aquinas' own, if immature, thought, than these later commentaries which were the product of his mature period.

Nevertheless, in that mature period there are sources which may be safely consulted with a view to ascertaining Aquinas' position on the problem of civil authority; indeed these mature sources must be consulted. In addition to certain references in his Summa Contra Gentiles,[233] the Summa Theologiae itself contains what has been referred to as his "Treatise on Law."[234]

The Problem of Civil Authority in the Later Writings

The Reaffirmation of Basic Themes

Many commentators have emphasized that a basic theme in Aquinas' view of civil authority is that the state derives from the nature of man.[235] That is, in accordance with Aristotelian principles, man in his essential nature is a political animal. Hence, the existence of civil authority is a natural condition, not a mere convention imposed on man in his corrupted state, with no inherent positive value of its own. However, in the sentential commentary Aquinas' endorsement of this principle is largely a matter of inference. In his later writings, however, Aquinas explicitly accepts the concept.

---

[233]See particularly, Summa de Veritate Catholicae Fidei Contra Gentiles, Book III, ch. 1, 81; Book IV, ch. 76. [Hereinafter referred to as "SCG".]

[234]See, e.g., Daniel A. Degnan, "Two Models of Positive Law in Aquinas: A Study of the Relationship of Positive Law and Natural Law," The Thomist 46 (January 1982): 1 and note 1. For a thorough study of natural law in light of the modern tradition of "analytical jurisprudence," see generally, John Finnis, Natural Law and Natural Rights (Oxford: Clarendon Press, 1980).

[235]A.P. d'Entreves, The Medieval Contribution to Political Thought (Oxford: Oxford University Press, 1939), p. 23.

Thus, in the De regimine principum we are told from the first that man is a "social and political animal" by nature,[236] and hence naturally and by necessity comes to live in a human community. Political life is therefore natural, since "it is natural for man to live in the society of many."[237]

Likewise, in considering the question of whether man in the "state of innocence" would be dominated by man, a question also considered in the sentential commentary,[238] the Summa Theologiae states that some form of dominion would obtain even there since "man is naturally a social animal."[239] Being social by nature, man would naturally live in a society. This condition would necessitate some minimal degree of organization and hence a minimal degree of directive authority. Relying expressly on the Politics, the Summa also insists that "since man is by nature a political animal,"[240] there is necessarily not only a rational and a divine order, but also a political order. Similarly, in attempting a classification of human law, the Summa recognizes that certain principles of human law can be viewed as deriving from natural law, "since man is by nature a social animal,"[241] so that essential norms in human law reflect this nature.

---

[236]De regimine principum, Book 1, ch. 1 (animal sociale et politicum).

[237]Ibid. (Est igitur homini naturale, quod in societate multorum vivat.)

[238]II Scriptum super Libros Sent. 44,1,3.

[239]Summa Theologiae [hereinafter "ST"], I, Q. 96, a. 4, Respondeo. (Quia homo naturaliter est animal sociale.)

[240]ST, I-II, Q. 72, a. 4, Respondeo. (Quia homo est naturaliter animal politicum et sociale.) The reference to the Politics is to Book 1, ch. 2, 1253a2.

[241]ST, I-II, Q. 95, a. 4, Respondeo. (Quia homo est naturaliter animal sociale.)

It is important to realize, however, that Aquinas' explicit reference to Aristotle does not necessarily entail the view that the former's political philosophy is simply a replication of the latter's. It is Aquinas' philosophical system which is assimilating principles of Aristotle's system into itself, not the other way around. It need hardly be emphasized that Aquinas' philosophical project is a creative one, and the result is to stand on its own merits.

The nature of the assimilation of Aristotle that is undertaken here can be understood even at a purely technical level. While it is obvious that Aquinas draws inspiration from Aristotle in positing the social and political nature of man, there is no literal transposition of the Aristotelian concept here. To the contrary, in a subtle manner, Aquinas has broadened the concept within his own philosophy. As d'Entreves has noted,[242] the Aristotelian term πολιτικὸν ζῶον may be rendered literally in Latin as animal civile, and this is the translation that William of Moerbeke gives in his translation of the Politics. Aquinas maintains this usage in his commentary on that work.[243] However, "the words animal sociale et politicum are constantly used in the Summa Theologica and in several other works relating to politics."[244] This philological detail suggests that Aquinas had expanded upon the Aristotelian concept which was his original inspiration.[245]

There is no mere replication here. The concept of the social and political nature of man gives Aquinas not only a basis for asserting the inherent necessity and positive value of the political life.

---

[242]d'Entreves, Medieval Contribution, p. 25, note 1.

[243]Not, however, in the Commentary on the Nicomachean Ethics. See, e.g., Book 1, Lecture 1 (animal sociale).

[244]d'Entreves, Medieval Contribution, p. 25, note 1.

[245]Cf., ibid., pp. 25-26.

(This was in any event more of an issue for the medieval Christian world than for the classical.[246]) It also gives him a basis, in the essential nature of man, for asserting a conceptual continuity with respect to the natural and human principles of law.[247] Thus, Aquinas' acceptance and transformation of this concept illustrates his creative assimilation of Aristotelian principles. It is in such developments that we may see the way in which Aquinas' philosophical undertaking "produced a fusion of Christian and Aristotelian themes."[248]

Thus, in asserting the essentially political and social nature of man, a principle already implied in his sentential commentary, Aquinas expands upon the Aristotelian principles which he assimilates in conformity with his own philosophical vision. In this regard, one commentator has noted:

> The Aristotelian teleology regarding the operations of nature and the idea of the State as a product of nature reappeared in the Thomist system; and so did the Aristotelian definition of man as a "political animal", which Thomas improved by designating man also as a social animal, so that his definition was expanded to man being "a political and social animal. . . . The concept of man as a political animal signified the entry of the "political" into contemporary vocabulary and thought-processes.[249]

---

[246]See, e.g., ibid., p. 33: The problem of obedience to civil authority "assumed in Christian political theory an importance unknown to the classical world."

[247]See, e.g., ST, I-II, Q. 95, a. 4, concerning the classifications of human law.

[248]Walter Ullmann, A History of Political Thought: The Middle Ages (Baltimore: Penguin Books, 1968), p. 174.

[249]Ibid., p. 175.

As to the nature of civil authority itself, we have seen that in the sentential commentary its distinguishing characteristic was that it was a principle of "order" in society. This characteristic was, in fact, at the heart of its inherent positive value. It continues as an essential feature in Aquinas' later writings. Thus, we are told in the *Summa Contra Gentiles* that "there is order to be found among men."[250] Any lack of order in human affairs would, it may be argued, reflect a lack of proper *ordering* among men. "Disorder results from the fact that someone presides, not because of preeminence of intellect but because he has seized civil power through violence, or is chosen to rule by swaying the passions of the people."[251] It is in disorder that civil power betrays its essential character.

Similarly, in the *Summa Theologiae* Aquinas argues that the order inherent to civil authority is itself inherent to the natural condition of man.[252]

---

[250] SCG, Book III, ch. 81 (*inter ipsos homines ordo invenitur*).

[251] Ibid. (*inordinatio provenit ex eo quod non propter intellectus praeminentiam aliquis praeest, sed vel robore corporali dominium sibi usurpat vel propter sensualem affectionem aliquis ad regendum praeficitur*).

[252] This principle is also endorsed by Professor Yves Simon in his 1940 Aquinas Lecture as a basic issue in defining the nature of authority. See Yves Simon, *Nature and Functions of Authority* (Milwaukee: Marquette University Press, 1948), pp. 1-14, passim: "Social happiness is based upon a felicitous combination of authority and liberty. . . . [A]uthority and liberty are at the same time antinomic and complementary terms. . . . [B]oth unrestricted liberty and boundless authority are fictitious conceptions, each of which implies its own negation together with the annihilation of society. . . . [T]he essential question, for every social group, is that of combining rightly the forces of authority and liberty. . . . The question is now whether authority has any essential function; whether the necessity of authority always results from some deficiency; whether authority, when necessary, is

A certain sort of subjection of one man to another is natural to man considered in himself, "for it would argue a lack of the good of order in the human community[253] if it were not governed by those who were wiser."[254] Again, in arguing whether there would have been dominion in the state of innocence (the paradigm condition for observing man's essential nature), Aquinas looks to Aristotle, in the first book of the Politics,[255] and to Augustine, in the De civitate Dei,[256] both used as auctoritates,

---

necessary solely on the ground of some defect in the one who is subjected to it." This question is, of course, at the heart of Aquinas' examination of the nature of civil authority. As we have argued, he rejects the view that authority has no essential function, that it exists only in light of the deficiencies of man's corrupted nature.

[253] In humana multitudine. The "multitude" or group, by the very fact of its multiplicity, appears to require an organizing principle, here civil authority. Cf. Simon, p. 17: The essential function of authority is "to assure the unity of action of a united multitude. A multitude aiming at a common good which can be attained only through a common action, must be united in its action by some steady principle. This principle is precisely what we call authority."

[254] ST, I, Q. 92, a. 1, ad 2 (defuisset enim bonum ordinis in humana multitudine, si quidam per alios sapientiores gubernati non fuissent).

[255] In Book 1, ch. 1, of the Politics, Aristotle emphasizes that, where a plurality directs itself to one object, there must be one in authority giving direction. This theme is repeated by Aquinas in Book 1, Lecture 1 of his Commentary on the Politics, and a similar theme is presented in the Proemium of his Commentary on the Metaphysics of Aristotle, with respect to the need for one science which "orders" the other sciences.

[256] De civitate Dei 19:15.

for the principle that some minimal form of dominion is part of the natural order (naturalis ordo) prescribed by God.257

Indeed, it is in this notion of order as an essential characteristic of civil authority that one finds its connection to Aquinas' conception of law. "Law strictly understood looks first and foremost to the ordering of the common good."258 Furthermore, this notion of order suggests an analogy between the natural order and human society, between natural law and human law:

> Just as in the natural order, divinely established, the inferior in natural things must necessarily be subject to the motion of the superior, so also in human affairs the inferior are required to obey their superiors, from the order of natural and divine law.259

The notion of ordering is thus retained in Aquinas' later writings as an essential characteristic of civil power. The concept is more extensively developed, however, and is linked to Aquinas' analysis of the nature of law.

257See ST, I, Q. 96, a. 4, Respondeo.

258ST, I-II, Q. 90, a. 3, Respondeo (lex proprie, primo et principaliter respicit ordinem ad bonum commune). There is a connection here to Aquinas' definition of law, in article 4 of the same question, "the rational ordering of things that concern the common good." (Legis [est] nihil . . . aliud quam quaedam rationis ordinatio ad bonum commune, ab eo qui curam communitatis habet, promulgata.)

259ST, II-II, Q. 104, a. 1, Respondeo (Et ideo sicut ex ipso ordine naturali divinitus instituto, inferiora in rebus naturalibus necesse habent subdi motioni superiorum, ita etiam in rebus humanis ex ordine iuris naturalis et divini, tenentur inferiores suis superioribus obedire).

The Natural Order among Men

What, then, is the natural order among men? Put in another way, if man is essentially a social and political animal, and if his social grouping is naturally characterized by order, how is this order expressed in practice? Is this order expressed in coercive relations between superior and inferior, or otherwise?

Even under the conventional view of civil authority, it must be admitted, there is some semblance of order, but it is imposed and coercive. Aquinas acknowledges in the Summa Contra Gentiles that coercive social relationships do reflect order. The apparent lack of order in the domination of the usurper itself is not ex-cluded from divine providence. It "emerges with divine permission on account of the defects of inferior agents."[260] Yet coercive order is not the fundamental order affirmed by Aquinas in the passages referred to in the previous section. Coercive order is to be compared with servitude, and it cannot be said to be a natural condition of man as man.[261] Rather, Aquinas is primarily concerned with a fundamental relationship which is natural to man, such that even "in the state of innocence, man could have exercised dominion over man."[262]

In Aquinas' later writings, then, we are faced with the question of the inherent positive value of civil authority once again. What is at stake is the underlying philosophical justification for Aquinas' assertion to the King of Cyprus to the effect that

> If . . . a community of free men is commanded by the ruler for the common

---

[260]SCG, Book III, ch. 81: Huiusmodi autem inordinatio divinam providentiam non excludit; provenit enim ex permissione divina, propter defectum inferiorum agentium.

[261]See ST, I, Q. 96, a. 4, Respondeo.

[262]Ibid. (in statu innocentiae, homo homini dominari potuisset).

>good, the governance will be fitting and just,[263]

whereas the conventional view of civil authority sees no civil power as fitting for truly free men, but only for those existing in a corrupted state. Hence, the test case for Aquinas' position in his later writings is the same as was found in the sentential commentary, namely, the postulated state of innocence.

In the *Summa Theologiae*, therefore, it will be his contention that "not even in the state of innocence was inequality of men excluded."[264] In this regard, the *Summa* virtually repeats the argumentation of the sentential commentary on the question of whether in the state of innocence there would have been some minimal degree of civil power. He distinguishes between those forms of dominion which are to be likened to servitude, and retains that form of dominion which arises, without oppression or coercion, out of man's social nature. If man is social by nature, and hence would be social in the state of inno-cence (posited as the natural state of man), then control of one by another may take place in the nature of direction toward the individual or common good,[265] because

>there could be no social existence of a community unless someone presided

---

[263]*De regimine principum*, Book 1, ch. 1. (*Si igitur liberorum multitudo a regente ad bonum commune multitudinis ordinetur, erit regimen rectum et iustum*.) Likewise, he instructs the Duchess of Brabant that "Princes of the earth are established by God . . . that they may procure for the people the common welfare." *De regimine Judaeorum*, ad 6 (*Principes terrarum sunt a Deo instituti . . . ut communem populi utilitatem procurent.*)

[264]ST, I, Q. 92, a. 1, ad 2. (*Nec inaequalitas hominum excluditur per innocentiae statum*. . . .)

[265]ST, I, Q. 96, a. 4, *Respondeo*. (*Ad proprium bonum eius . . . vel ad bonum commune*.

> there could be no social existence of a community unless someone presided with a view toward the common good.[266]

Thus, Aquinas isolates a natural conception of civil authority, possessing a positive value, quite detached from the preoccupation of the conventional view of civil authority with the problem of evil. In this regard Morrall has stated that for Aquinas

> The use of such leadership for the common good would have been necessary even without the fall [of man from the posited state of innocence]; here Thomas tacitly parts company with the old patristic tradition of the conventional character of political authority. St. Thomas regards political life as an essential feature of man's original and therefore natural condition.[267]

In observing the development of Aquinas' thought, it is significant that, in the *Summa*, the choice of the natural view of civil authority over the conventional view is, as Morrall observes, "tacit." Unlike the sentential commentary, which is reacting at least in a general way to the structure and content of Lombard's text, the parallel discussion in the *Summa* concerning the status of civil authority in the state of innocence does not explicitly cite the alternative status advocated by the conventional view. The analysis presented by the *Summa* is, even on this textual level, an independent creative effort on the part of Aquinas.

As has already been implied, however, Aquinas' mature analysis of the nature of civil authority retains many of the fundamental choices of principle

---

[266]Ibid. (*Socialis autem vita multorum esse non posset, nisi aliquis praesideret, qui ad bonum commune intenderet.*)

[267]John B. Morrall, *Political Thought in Medieval Times* (New York: Harper Torchbooks, 1962), p. 72.

initiated in the sentential commentary. Primary among these is the distinction drawn in the Summa's discussion of the state of innocence between civil power which is coercive, in thenature of servitude, with a more benign sense of civil power, in the nature of direction. This distinction is the same as that drawn in the sentential commentary between the "coercive" and "guiding" modes of sovereignty. The distinction is crucial to Aquinas' position, since it is the latter sense or mode which he will claim as natural to man as a political and social animal, even in the state of nature.

The emphasis upon the guiding mode of civil power is a consistent feature throughout the later writings. It is repeatedly asserted in the De regimine principum. From the first page, Aquinas notes that "man needs a certain guidance toward [his] end."[268] Guidance in fact defines the concept of governance.[269]

This theme is, of course, picked up in the Summa's discussion of the state of innocence, and it is frequently repeated. Thus, we are told that "governance is nothing other than the direction of the governed to an end, which is a certain good."[270] Again, in considering the moral object of the law, the Summa states that "it is fitting for the law to induce the subjects to their own virtue."[271] Similarly, in its treatment of the essential characteristics of the law, for purposes of its proper classification, the Summa identifies, among others, the following two:

---

[268]De regimine principum, Book 1, ch. 1. (Indiget igitur homo aliquo dirigente ad finem.)

[269]Ibid., ch. 14. (Gubernare est, id quod gubernatur convenienter ad debitum finem perfucere.)

[270]ST, I, Q. 103, a. 3, Respondeo. (Gubernatio nihil aliud est quam directio gubernatorum ad finem, qui est aliquod bonum.)

[271]ST, I-II, Q. 92, a. 1, Respondeo. (Sit proprium legis, inducere subiectos ad propriam ipsorum virtutem.)

that it be established by the ruler of the civil community . . . [and] that it be directive of human actions.272

Hence, the analysis of the natural order among men presented in the sentential commentary is reaffirmed in the later writings of Aquinas. The essence of civil authority is order, and not merely coercive order but order that is established through the directive activity of the sovereign in the interests of the common good. There remains to be assessed the extent and limits of obedience owed to those invested with civil authority, the last major issue of the sentential commentary.

The Limits of Civil Obedience

In the sentential commentary, the question of the limits of the duty of obedience to civil authority was raised in the context of an analysis of the nature of obedience itself, including three questions: (i) whether it was a virtue; (ii) whether Christians were required to obey secular authorities; and, (iii) whether religious were required to obey their prelates in all things. The discussion was still rooted in a moral, and indeed theological setting. While the discussion in his later writings on the same subject, and particularly in the Summa Theologiae, retains the moral implications of the earlier analysis, its setting is more broadly philosophical. This setting may be grasped by considering the Summa's parallel text to the commentary's discussion of obedience to secular rulers. In Quaestio 104 of the Secunda Secundae, the fifth article asks whether subjects (subditi), not "Christians," are required to obey their superiors (suis superioribus), not "secular authorities."

272ST, I-II, Q. 95, a. 4, Respondeo. (Tertio est de ratione legis humanae ut instituatur a gubernante communitatem civitatis. . . . Quarto vero de ratione legis humanae est quod sit directiva humanorum actuum. The other two essential characteristics of human law are that it be derived (derivata) from natural law, and that it be directed to the common good (ordinetur ad bonum commune).

In the Respondeo to this article, Aquinas endorses obedience to civil authority as the norm of the political community, and he identifies two situations in which the duty does not obtain. First, there may be a contrary command of a higher power.[273] Second, obedience is not required "if the superior commands something of the subject in which the latter is not subordinated to him."[274] It is only after these general philosophical precepts are established on the question of obedience that Aquinas introduces in the sixth article the question earlier considered in the sentential commentary, namely, the question of whether the Christian is required to obey secular authorities.[275] Here Aquinas reaches essentially the same conclusion, following from virtually the same sort of argumentation, as was found in the sentential commentary. The liberation of faith does not destroy civil obligations. To conclude otherwise would be to subvert civil order, that essential feature of civil authority wherein its positive value is located. Aquinas observes:

> The order of justice requires that subjects obey their superiors. Otherwise, the stability of human affairs could not be preserved. Hence, the faithful are not excused through faith in Christ from the requirement that they obey secular princes.[276]

What, then, of the problematic case of the obedience due to a tyrant or usurper? In writing to

---

[273]ST, II-II, Q. 104, a. 5, Respondeo (propter praeceptum maioris potestatis).

[274]Ibid. (si ei aliquid praecipiat in quo ei non subdatur).

[275]Cf. II Scriptum super Libros Sent. 44,2,2 and ST, II-II, Q. 104, a. 6.

[276]ST, II-II, Q. 104, a. 6, Respondeo. (Ordo autem iustitiae requirit ut inferiores suis superioribus obediant: aliter enim non posset humanarum rerum status conservari.)

the King of Cyprus, Aquinas is somewhat guarded in his comments. At times it may appear that he suggests an attitude of endurance, in keeping with the conventional view of civil authority.[277] Similarly, as we have seen in the Summa Contra Gentiles, Aquinas notes that the disorder apparent in the rule of the usurper "is not excluded" by divine providence.[278]

Ultimately, though these remarks may be ambiguous, his mature view does seem to urge tolerance of the reign of the tyrant in most cases. Even the authority of the tyrant may partake of the essential characteristics of true authority, thus requiring obedience. In his discussion of the moral object of law in the Summa Theologiae, we read:

> Tyrannical law . . . is not really law, but a perversion of law. Still, insofar as it does partake of the essence of law, . . . it is the dictate of one in authority to his subjects. . . .[279]

Furthermore, in terms of its derivation from divine law (the source of its legitimacy), human law which deviates from reason, as tyrannical law does, "does not possess the essence of law, but rather that of violence."[280] Is such "law" legitimate? Citing Romans 13:1, Aquinas affirms that in a certain sense it is legitimate:

---

[277]See, e.g., De regimine principum, Book 1, ch. 9: Et ipse Deus mala esse in mundo non sineret, nisi ex eis bona eliceret ad utilitatem et pulchritudinem universi.

[278]See SCG, Book III, ch. 81.

[279]ST, I-II, Q. 92, a. 1, ad 4 (lex tyrannica . . . non est simpliciter lex, sed magis est quaedam perversitas legis. Et tamen inquantum habet aliquid de ratione legis, . . . est dictamen alicuius praesidentis in subditis. . . .

[280]ST, I-II, Q. 93, a. 3, ad 3 (et sic non habet rationem legis, sed magis violentiae cuiusdam.)

> in this unjust law, insofar as it retains the appearance of law, on account of the authority of him who issues the law, in this respect it is still derived from the eternal law. . . .[281]

Thus, to the extent that the essential relationship of an ordering of human affairs through the authority of a superior still obtains under the tyrant, he is apparently to be tolerated. It may be in part on account of such passages that one commentator has emphasized the extraordinary patience that Aquinas seems to urge:

> a king will find himself well rewarded if he carries [the responsibilities of kingship] out. But what happens if he does not? This is the subject's problem. . . . The answer invariably found is that the subject must bear injustice and tyranny with patience.[282]

It is true that Aquinas looks to the ordering of superior and inferior as an essential feature of civil authority. And so, even as a remedy for tyrannical rule, he is hesitant to hazard the disorder which may be attendant upon active resistance to any civil power. While his remarks to the King of Cyprus may be influenced by that reader's station, his concern seems genuine:

> It would be dangerous for the human community and for its rulers if some on private initiative were to attempt the death of those who preside, even if they be tyrants.[283]

---

[281]Ibid. (Et tamen in ipsa lege iniqua inquantum servatur aliquid de similtudine legis propter ordinem potestatis eius qui legem facit, secundum hoc etiam derivatur a lege aeterna. . . .)

[282]Jean Dunbabin, "Aristotle in the Schools," in Trends in Medieval Political Thought, ed. Beryl Smalley (Oxford: Basil Blackwell, 1965), p. 77.

[283]De regimine principum, Book 1, ch. 6.

Rather, the apparent disorder of rule by a tyrant or usurper is best remedied in his view not by private initiative (<u>privata presumptione</u>) but by public process, if this is at all possible. He goes on to say:

It appears that one ought to proceed against the evils of tyranny not by private initiative of some persons, but by public authority. First, if it pertains to the right of the community to provide itself with a king, it would not be unjust to depose the king or restrict his power if it be abused tyrannically.[284]

Likewise, where the ruler is not elected but appointed by some higher authority, then "the remedy is to be sought from him."[285] Thus, contrary to the view of the commentator quoted above, Aquinas is not simply relegating the subject to patience and endurance of tyrannical rule. He urges, however, that orderly procedures, where they exist, be utilized to vindicate the orderliness that is essential to civil authority. Nevertheless, at least in the remarks to the King of Cyprus, Aquinas concludes that where such orderly procedures are not available, "one must have recourse to God, the king of all,"[286] in the apparent hope that divine

---

(<u>Esset autem hoc multitudini periculosum et eius rectoribus, si privata praesumptione aliqui attentarent praesidentium necem, etiam tyrannorum.</u>)

[284]Ibid. (<u>Videtur autem magis contra tyrannorum saevitiam non privata praesumptione aliquorum, sed auctoritate publica procedendum. Primo quidem, si ad ius multitudinis alicuius pertineat sibi providere de rege, non iniuste ab eadem rex institutus potest destrui vel refrenari eius potestas, si potestate regia tyrannice abutatur.</u>)

[285]Ibid. (<u>expectandum est ab [superiore] remedium contra tyranni nequitiam</u>). Thus, here as in the sentential commentary, Aquinas implies that subjects have a right to petition higher civil authorities.

[286]Ibid. (<u>recurrendum est ad regem omnium Deum</u>).

providence may soften the heart of the tyrant. This is, of course, ultimately unsatisfying as a resolution of the problem of tyrannical rule. The sentential commentary would go further than this.

This is not, however, the ultimate resolution of the problem as we find it in the Summa Theologiae. There Aquinas' discussion of the binding force of human law notes that laws which are unjust, either because they are detrimental to the common welfare, because they were promulgated in excess of the sovereign's authority, or because they are otherwise inequitable, are binding only as a matter of prudence. "Such laws do not obligate man as a matter of conscience, except perhaps to avoid scandal or disturbance."[287] However, laws which are unjust because they are directly contrary to divine law "are in no way to be observed."[288] We may see here a direct parallel to the analysis in the sentential commentary of the duty to obey civil authority where the authority is defective because of its abusive exercise.[289]

This parallel is reinforced in the Summa's discussion of resistance to tyrants. The issue is framed in terms of the moral question whether resistance, even to tyrannical government, constitutes the sin of sedition.[290] Here again Aquinas' analysis turns on the concept of order as the essential feature of civil authority.

---

[287]ST, I-II, Q. 96, a. 4, Respondeo. (Unde tales leges non obligant in foro conscientiae: nisi forte propter vitandum scandalum vel turbationem. . . .) To similar effect is the later discussion of the proper interpretation of human law. See, e.g., ibid., a. 6, Respondeo: omnis lex ordinatur ad communem hominum salutem, et intanto obtinet vim et rationem legis; secundum vero quod ab hoc deficit, virtutem obligandi non habet.

[288]ST, I-II, Q. 96, a. 4, Respondeo. (Et tales leges nullo modo licet observare. . . .)

[289]See II Scriptum super Libros Sent. 44,2,2, Solutio.

[290]ST, II-II, Q. 42, a. 2.

Tyrannical government is unjust because it is not ordained (non ordinatur) towards the common good, but towards the private good of the ruler. Hence, overthrow of such a government is not in essence sedition (non habet rationem seditionis). Having stated this conclusion, however, Aquinas does immediately qualify it. The overthrow of such a government is permissible,

> except perhaps where . . . the community suffers a greater detriment from the consequent disturbance than from the rule of the tyrant.[291]

Thus, we are returned to the cautious expressions of the need for prudence which we earlier encountered in Aquinas' remarks to the King of Cyprus. We may therefore be justified in concluding that those remarks do in fact represent Aquinas' thought accurately, despite the audience for which they were intended.

V. BONAVENTURE'S SENTENTIAL COMMENTARY

In juxtaposition to Aquinas' analysis of the problem of civil authority, and particularly the analysis in his own sentential commentary, how does Bonaventure's treatment compare? We have seen that Aquinas' approach to the problem seems creative and by no means a literal commentary. To what extent does Bonaventure's commentary evidence a similar degree of creativity? To what extent is he simply following out the implications of the Augustinian tradition,[292] and to what extent does he stand in

---

[291]Ibid. (nisi forte quando sic inordinate perturbatur tyranni regimen quod multitudo subiecta maius detrimentum patitur ex perturbatione consequenti, quam ex

[292]As Gilson has insisted, Bonaventure's training was decidedly in the Augustinian tradition. See E. Gilson, The Philosophy of St. Bonaventure, trans. I. Trethowan and F. J. Sheed (New York: Sheed & Ward, 1940), p. 5: "Between the years 1243 and

stand in stark opposition to Aquinas on the issues raised by the problem of civil authority? These are some of the questions which should be kept in mind as we proceed through the following comparative analysis of Bonaventure's sentential commentary.[293]

The Structure of the Commentary

Both in its general outline and internal structure, Bonaventure's sentential commentary is strikingly similar to that of Aquinas. Since the sentential commentary was an institutionalized prerequisite in the course of study at the University of Paris at the time that both writers,

---

1248 [Bonaventure] was initiated first by Alexander of Hales, then by Jean de la Rochelle, into an essentially Augustinian theology. . . ." Gilson has also emphasized that Bonaventure "set out in his Commentary on the Sentences, as early as the years 1250-1251, the totality of the philosophic and theological conceptions, Augustinian in inspiration, of which he was to remain thereafter the champion." Ibid., p. 6 (footnote omitted). See also Matthew M. De Benedictis, The Social Thought of Saint Bonaventure, The Catholic University of America Philosophical Series, vol. XCIII (Westport, Conn.: Greenwood Press, 1972), pp. 3-4, noting that, in terms of his sources, after the sacred scripture, Bonaventure "attaches the greatest moment to the writings of [St. Augustine]. Regarding the influence of St. Augustine on the writings of [Bonaventure] there is no doubt, for almost all are agreed as to the Augustinian character of his writings. . . . It was St. Augustine's De Civitate Dei that found an echo in St. Bonaventure's social doctrine." Bonaventure's own view of the value of his work was strikingly modest. He refers to himself as a "continuator" of the work of Alexander of Hales, his mentor. (See Liber II Sent. 23,2,3, ad finem.) While few students of his work would agree, he goes so far as to refer to himself as a "simple compiler." (See ibid., praelocutio.)

[293]A translation of Bonaventure's commentary of Distinction 44 of the Second Book of the Sentences appears in Part III, infra.

themselves contemporaries,[294] aspired to the <u>magister</u>, it is perhaps not entirely surprising that the formal structure of the two commentaries are so similar.

As in the case of Aquinas' commentary, Bonaventure's work is divided into three major parts. He begins with a section entitled "Textual Analysis."[295] The treatment here is literal and perfunctory, intended as little more than an outline of Lombard's text.

The second major part of the work constitutes the body of the commentary itself.[296] The technical divisions within this part do not precisely mirror Aquinas' divisions. Here the major division is the "Article" under which are arranged a series of "questions." Each "question" is, however, arranged along precisely the same lines as Aquinas' "article," namely, (i) a series of enumerated arguments taking one side of the issue raised by the question; (ii) a <u>Sed contra</u>, taking the opposite side of the issue; (iii) a <u>Respondeo</u>, setting forth Bonaventure's resolution of the problem;[297] and, (iv) a series of specific responses to the side of the argument not favored by the <u>Respondeo</u>.

One structural difference between Bonaventure's "question" and the "article" of Aquinas should be noted. The <u>Sed contra</u> in Aquinas' commentary is usually no more than a brief suggestion of a counterposition, consisting of no more than two paragraphs, sometimes with no citation of supporting authority. In the case of Bonaventure's commentary,

---

[294]Allan Wolter gives Bonaventure's dates as 1217-1274. See <u>The Encyclopedia of Philosophy</u>, 1972 Reprint ed., s.v. "Bonaventure," by Allan B. Wolter. Gilson gives the date 1221 as the year of his birth. See Gilson, p. 1.

[295]<u>Divisio Textus</u>. Aquinas' terminology is identical. Cf. Part II, text and accompanying note 2, infra, and Part III, text and accompanying note 2, infra.

[296]Bonaventure denominates the second part <u>Tractatio Quaestionum</u>.

however, the <u>Sed contra</u> is a fully developed set of arguments, set forth with as much detail and citation as one finds in the initial enumerated arguments themselves. Hence, the argumentation between conflicting positions often seems fuller than we are used to seeing in Aquinas' commentary. We must therefore inquire, as we proceed through our analysis of Bonaventure's commentary, concerning the extent to which Bonaventure's own position may be reflected in this full argumentation.

An outline of the issues raised by Bonaventure's sentential commentary also differs in certain respects from that of Aquinas, but neither confines itself at all closely to the outline of Lombard's own text. Bonaventure divides the commentary into three articles, each with its series of questions. The structure of the body of the commentary may therefore be represented in the following schematic fashion:

   I.   Origin of the power of sin

        A.   Whether it arises from God
        B.   Whether the power is evil

   II. Power for governing

        A.   Whether every such power comes from God
        B.   Whether it is a natural institution or a punishment

   III. Necessity for subjection to the governing power

        A.   Whether Christians are required to obey secular powers
        B.   Whether the religious must obey prelates in all things

---

[297]As is the case with Aquinas' <u>Solutio</u>, it is only in the <u>Respondeo</u> that we can safely locate Bonaventure's own views on the issues under discussion.

While there are certainly close parallels between the texts of Bonaventure and Aquinas, the differences in structure are also notable. The juxtaposition of the two texts, according to their respective schematic structures[298] may be represented as follows:

Aquinas	Bonaventure
IA	IA, B[299]
IB	IIA
IC	IIB
IIA[300]	----
IIB	IIIA
IIC	IIIB

Without overemphasizing these minor structural divergences, we cannot ignore the differences in approach which are evident from this graphic rendition of the respective structures of the two sentential commentaries. Note, for example, that Bonaventure considers, methodically, whether the power for sin arises from God, and then whether, understood in the way it is analyzed within the commentary, it is evil. In contrast, Aquinas appears to conflate these two issues. On the other hand, Bonaventure provides no parallel to Aquinas' treatment of the preliminary question of the nature of obedience itself before considering the question of whether one is required to obey certain specific types of authority.[301] However, what is probably most striking in this comparison of the structures of the two commentaries is the fact that, overall, the structures are so closely parallel in the first place.

---

[298]A schematic representation of the corresponding discussion in Aquinas' commentary is set forth in the text following note 130 supra.

[299]See text following note 314, infra.

[300]I.e., the question whether obedience is a virtue.

[301]One may be tempted to see the influence of Aristotle in Aquinas' insistence on examining this preliminary question, since much of the discussion concerns the question of whether or nor the concept

The third major part of Bonaventure's commentary is entitled "Doubts concerning the Writings of the Master." Despite the differences in title, it is in function quite similar to the third major part of Aquinas' commentary, entitled "Literal Exposition." Each raises a series of textual problems, discussed in the form of a literal commentary.[302]

The Substance of the Commentary

The first article of Bonaventure's commentary on Distinction 44 concerns the origin of the power of sin. As we have already seen, he divides this issue into two questions, first, whether or not this power arises in man from God, and second, whether the power, such as it is, is good or evil. Only the first of these questions has a direct parallel in Aquinas' commentary.[303]

The first question begins with a series of argu-ments in support of the proposition that the power for sin does arise in man from God. The first argument merely restates the position taken by Lombard, citing Augustine,[304] to the effect that it is

---

of obedience can be included under the Aristotelian definition of a virtue, and whether it is general or specific, a problem raised by Aristotle in considering the nature of the concept of justice. In this light, it is perhaps understandable that Bonaventure does not provide a distinct treatment of this issue within the context of his commentary on the problem of civil authority.

[302]The exception to this statement, of course, is the curious passage which is appended to the end of Aquinas' Literal Exposition, in which he considers, in the format of an <u>articulus</u>, whether a "superior" authority is to be obeyed to a greater extent than an "inferior" authority. There is little corresponding discussion in Bonaventure's commentary on Distinction 44 in the "Doubts." Cf. text at notes 384-386, infra.

[303]Cf. Aquinas, II <u>Scriptum super Libros Sent.</u> 44,1,1.

[304]<u>In Psalms</u> 32:3.

man's will for doing evil that arises from man, but it is without power except from God. The second argument refers to Aristotle for the curious proposition that "God and the zealot can do depraved things,"[305] or at any rate what might appear to be depraved. The argument goes on to state that, if man and God share this potential, man must partake of it from God.

The last three arguments shift their attention to a purely conceptual analysis of the notion of the power for sin in itself. For example, the third enumerated argument asserts that the power can be viewed as confirming the excellence of nature, since only the rational creature (the most excellent of creatures) is capable of sin. However, the argument proceeds, anything which confirms the excellence of nature is from God. Similarly, the fourth enumerated argument asserts that the power contributes to the praise of the just, for "to be capable of sin contributes to the praise of the just man,"[306] since he refrains from sin though he is capable of it. The argument then asserts that anything contributing to the amplication of praise is necessarily from God. Finally, the fifth enumerated argument presents the following reductio argument. This power in a rational creature is necessarily from God or from nothing. Assuming that it is not from God, and hence is from nothing, "then since every creatures comes from nothing, each has the potentiality for sin. If, then, this is false, the [first] proposition [i.e., that the power comes from God] remains."[307]

---

[305]The text here is problematic. See Part III, note 13, infra. In addition, the reference to Topics, Book IV, ch. 5 in Bonaventure's text seems misplaced.

[306]Bonaventure, Liber II Sent. 44,1,1,4, citing Ecclesiastes 31:10.

[307]Liber II Sent. 44,1,1,5.

Bonaventure's <u>Sed contra</u> adopts the contrary side of the argument, which is also supported by the enumerated arguments at the beginning of Aquinas' own discussion of the problem.[308] Few of the specific arguments have parallels in those of Aquinas. The <u>Sed contra</u> repeatedly emphasizes the defective character of sin, and links this defect or privation to the power for sin itself.[309] Given this defective nature, it is impossible, relying on Augustine,[310] to locate an exemplar in God for this power. Hence, it is not from God.

The second argument of the <u>Sed contra</u> does have an indirect parallel in the second enumerated argument of Aquinas' first article. Bonaventure's <u>Sed contra</u> argues:

> act and potential are from the same principle. Therefore, if sin is not from God in any way, then neither is the potential for sin in man from God.[311]

In somewhat similar fashion, Aquinas had presented an argument to the effect that act is more perfect than potency, and "since . . . the act of sin is not from God, neither will the potential for sin be from God."[312]

Bonaventure's resolution of these conflicting views in his <u>Respondeo</u>, like Aquinas' in his <u>Solutio</u>, ultimately turns upon an equivocal use of

---

[308] See II <u>Scriptum super Libros Sent.</u> 44,1,1,1-5.

[309] E.g., <u>Liber II Sent.</u> 44,1, <u>Sed contra</u> a. (priva-tion not from God); c. (grace perfects nature and removes power for sin); d. (potentiality for sin is potentiality for opposing God).

[310] See citations in Part III, note 16, infra.

[311] <u>Liber II Sent.</u> 44,1,1, <u>Sed contra</u> b.

[312] II <u>Scriptum super Libros Sent.</u> 44,1,1,2.

the term "power" or "potential." One may be referring either to the potential in itself ("as to what is potential") or to the inclination or direction of the potential towards sin ("a privation and a defect . . . nothing other than a deficiency"). Thus, one can accept Lombard's authorities in support of the proposition that the power is from God, but only on the supposition that one is referring to the potential in itself, not the deficiency of man's direction towards certain acts.

Hence, Bonaventure argues in response to the first enumerated argument that one may cite Augustine in support of the proposition that the potential comes from God, but not the will to sin. However, this proposition can only be accepted to the extent that one understands the potential as in itself. The disposition towards sin is a defect of our corrupt nature.

As to the citation to Aristotle in the second enumerated argument, Bonaventure simply and explicitly rejects it as false:

> some explain that the Philosopher was thinking of the evil that consists of punishment. But this is plainly inconsistent with his text. . . . I respond by saying that that passage from the Philosopher is bereft of truth.[313]

---

[313] Liber II Sent. 44,1,1, ad 2. This passage tends to support Gilson's observations concerning Bonaventure's attitude toward Aristotelianism. See Gilson, pp. 3-4: "But . . . it is important to realize that St. Bonaventure did not set out upon a way that would have led to Christian Aristotelianism if he had not stopped too soon. The truth is that from the first he had attached himself to a doctrine which was its radical negation. . . . One principal reason why this vital fact is not recognized is that his Commentary on the Sentences, which from end to end is wholly given to exposition to the exclusion of polemic, does not waste much time in direct criticism of Aristotle. But even here it is to be noticed that St. Bonaventure is not ignorant of Aristotle's teaching, and indeed that he frequently quotes his authority." While it may be argued that

Similarly, as to the three arguments based upon analysis of the concept of "power" itself, Bonaventure will not accept them, except to the extent that they rely upon reference to the first equivocal meaning of "power" (the potential for acting taken in itself). "[W]hen it is asked whether [the power] comes from God, it is not to be answered absolutely but in accordance with the [equivocal] distinction discussed above."[314]

It has already been mentioned that the problem of the source of the human capacity for sin represents one aspect of the problem of evil. In that regard it appears to have been an unstated assumption in Aquinas' discussion that placing the source of that capacity in God, but not the act of sin, was one strategy in resolving the problem of evil. Bonaventure does not leave this assumption unstated, nor is he content to assume the answer. Accordingly, the second question of the first article explicitly addresses the issue of whether the potential for sin, understood in the way developed in the previous question, is itself evil nevertheless. There is no parallel treatment in Aquinas' commentary.

The enumerated arguments which begin the question take the position that the potential is evil. In a sense, much of the argumentation resurrects the discussion of the previous question. Thus, the first argument here asserts that the potential "is nothing other than the will."[315] The will for sin is evil, and so also the potential.

The second argument is particularly familiar:

> anything the use of which is evil, is also itself evil. But the use of the

---

Bonaventure's sentential commentary is not so simply expository, it cannot be denied that his opposition to Aristotelian principles is clear, both from the text quoted above and from the remainder of the commentary as well.

[314] <u>Liber II Sent.</u> 44,1,1, ad 5.

[315] <u>Liber II Sent.</u> 44,1,2,1.

> potential for sin is sin, and to sin
> is evil. And therefore the potential
> for sin is evil.[316]

This is precisely the same argument as that found in the fifth enumerated argument of Aquinas' first article. Thus, it should be clear that Bonaventure is in fact separating out for explicit discussion an aspect of the broader issue of the source of the potential for sin. Whereas Bonaventure expressly draws from this argument (not necessarily as an expression of his own view, of course) the conclusion that the potential is evil, this conclusion remains unstated but assumed in Aquinas' presentation of the same argument.[317]

That this present question is a direct development from the previous question is also evident from the fifth enumerated argument. This directly parallels the fifth argument of the previous Sed contra, concerning the impossibility of the existence of a divine exemplar of the power for sin. In the present discussion, Bonaventure presents the following argument:

> the potential for doing evil is
> either good or bad. If it is good
> .... then ... the potential
> ... both comes from and exists in
> God, both of which are false. Hence,
> it remains that the potential for sin
> is evil.[318]

The Sed contra in the second question of course takes the position that the potential for sin is not evil. It begins with a reductio argument to the effect that to say that the potential for sin is itself evil is to say that anyone who is capable of sin is evil. The result would be that the just and

---

[316]Ibid., 44,1,2,2. The import of the third enumerated argument is similar.

[317]Similarly, Bonaventure's fourth enumerated argu-ment parallels the second argument in Aquinas' first article. Both argue that the act is more perfect/complete than its corresponding potential, and hence, if the act is evil, so also the less perfect/complete potential.

and holy man is evil, a proposition which the argument by implication rejects.[319]

The problem of evil, and the explanation of its existence as a punishment imposed on man, is perhaps implied in the second argument of the Sed contra:

> if the potential for sin is evil, then it is by way of either an evil of punishment or an evil of deliberate fault or guilt. It is not the former, because that follows the latter. It is not the latter, because fault or guilt is the consequent of the potential for sin in time and by nature. Yet both man and angel could sin prior to either sinning.[320]

Bonaventure's resolution of this question is again based upon a distinction. The direction of the will toward evil is an action, and is evil ("direction in the sense of an action"). To the contrary, the potential for action, considered in itself in the manner suggested by the Respondeo of the previous question, is merely a capacity ("direction . . . in the sense of a state"). Hence, with regard to the latter, one is not said to be actually directing oneself (i.e., one's will) toward evil, merely on the strength of the capacity alone. Hence, Bonaventure concedes the truth of the position presented by the arguments in the Sed contra.

Thus, as to the specific enumerated arguments which opened the discussion, Bonaventure rejects the underlying assumption that the will and the potential (capacity) for action are the same.[321]

---

[318]Liber II Sent. 44,1,2,5.

[319]Ibid., 44,1,2, Sed contra, a. See also, ibid., 44,1,2, Sed contra, c-d.

[320]Ibid., Sed contra, b.

[321]Ibid., 44,1,2, ad 1.

Similarly, he refuses to accept the identification of the potential for action (taken in itself) with a specific activation of that potential, here in the act of sin.[322] The activation of the potential in the act of sin is a defective use of the potential and does not define it. "Hence the opposite of sin is [the potential's proper] use and sin is its abuse."[323]

Similarly, he rejects the argument that the potential for sin is "completed" in the act of sin and thus shares evil with it as an element. The potential is "completed" only "as to the act to which it is ordained absolutely. But it is not true of that to which it is ordained accidentally, especially when that act is understood more under the concept of a defect than of an effect."[324]

It is in the second article that Bonaventure first addresses the problem of civil authority directly. This article carries the title "Concerning the power for governing" (De potestate praesidendi), and it is in the philosophical analysis which follows that we may notice a certain lack of technical precision. Bonaventure alternates between the use of the term "governing" and "ruling" with no apparent difference in the intended meaning.[325] In contrast, Aquinas is careful to distinguish between a power for "guiding" (ad regimen ordinatus) and "dominating" (ad dominandum), and the distinction is of crucial significance in his analysis.[326]

---

[322]Ibid., 44,1,2, ad 2.

[323]Ibid. See also ibid., 44,1,2, ad 3: In the act of sin, "although the potential cannot perfect itself through its act, still it can disorder itself through its act."

[324]Ibid., 44,1, ad 4. See also ibid., ad 5.

[325]See, e.g., Part III, text and accompanying note 36, infra (omnis potentia dominandi); text and accompanying notes 37-38 (potestas dominandi); text and accompanying note 42 (potestate praesidendi).

[326]Bonaventure seems similarly unconcerned with any technical apparatus for distinguishing shades of

Nevertheless, in substance Bonaventure's analysis of the problem is noteworthy. In the first question under the present article, Bonaventure considers whether every potential for ruling comes from God. This corresponds to Aquinas' discussion in his first question, second article.

Bonaventure begins with a series of enumerated arguments in support of the position that every such power is from God. The first half of the series is scriptural in its inspiration, citing Christ's colloquy with Pilate and the classic text of Romans 13:1.[327] The second half of the series is more conceptual. Echoing an argument from the first question of the first article,[328] the third enumerated argument states that this power is in the nature of an excellence, an affirmation. Hence, since every affirmation comes from the highest power (a summa potentia), this potential necessarily comes from God.[329] Bonaventure cites no authority for this argument.

The fourth enumerated argument alludes to the conventional view of civil authority. Punishment comes from God, and the power for ruling, like servitude, is imposed as a punishment.[330] What is curious about this argument, presented without citation, is that it assumes the conventional view and uses that assumption as a basis for urging the source of authority in God. One would expect the conventional view itself to be presented as an explanation of how it is that the source of authority is to be located in God, with the latter proposition often being the one which is assumed.[331]

---

meaning, in Latin, for the corresponding English term "power." Cf. e.g., Part III, notes 35-38, 42-43, 46, infra.

[327]Liber II Sent. 44,2,1,1-2.

[328]Cf. ibid., 44,1,1,3.

[329]Ibid., 44,2,1,3.

[330]Ibid., 44,2,1,4.

[331]See generally Walter Ullmann, A History of Political Thought: The Middles Ages (Baltimore:

117

The *Sed contra* here takes the position that civil power is not from God. Many of the arguments presented here are precise parallels to the enumerated arguments of Aquinas' discussion in the first question, second article, of his commentary. Thus, the first argument of the *Sed contra* cites the scriptural passage, "They have set up kings, but not by me,"[332] just as we find in the first enumerated argument of Aquinas' discussion.[333]

The second argument of the *Sed contra* points to the unjust rule of many sovereigns, whereas nothing unjust can be said to come from God. This generally parallels the second enumerated argument of Aquinas' discussion, which relies upon the assertion that "whatever is done perversely is not from God."[334] Both texts also present arguments based on the assertion that what is from God is essentially ordered, whereas disorder in relations is often the norm between sovereign and subjects, with the foolish over the wise.[335] Both present empirical arguments to the effect that sovereigns are in fact overthrown, whereas what comes from God cannot be usurped.[336]

However, it is Bonaventure, and not Aquinas, who invokes the priniciple of natural law in the context of the present argument. Relying upon the *Institutes* of Justinian,[337] the argument proceeds as follows:

> nothing that is contrary to natural law is from God. But the power for

---

Penguin Books, 1968), pp. 120-2.

[332]Hosea 8:4.

[333]See II *Scriptum super Libros Sent.* 44,1,2,1.

[334]*Ibid.*, 44,1,2,2.

[335]Cf. *ibid.*, 44,1,2,5 and *Liber II Sent.* 44,2,1, *Sed contra*, c.

[336]Cf. II *Scriptum super Libros Sent.* 44,1,2,3-4 and *Liber II Sent.* 44,2,1, *Sed contra*, e-f.

[337]Book 1, 2:2.

nothing that is contrary to natural law is from God. But the power for ruling over men is contrary to natural law. Therefore it is not from God. . . . The minor [premise] is proven by what is written in the Institutes, "Wars have arisen, and captivity and slavery have followed, which are contrary to natural law."[338]

Bonaventure's Respondeo is also strikingly similar to Aquinas' Solutio on this issue. Bonaventure distinguishes the capacity for governing itself, which he concedes is from God, from the mode of acquiring or retaining the position of sovereignty.[339] The mode may vary; "some preside over others out of justice, some from cunning, and some from violence."[340] In the first case, when the mode corresponds to the essential capacity, "then that power for ruling . . . is from God."[341] In the latter two cases, however, further distinctions are required.

Bonaventure appears to agree with Aquinas on the principle that sovereignty is from God, insofar as it partakes of the essential capacity (or form) of governing, even in problematic cases (i.e., where it is acquired or retained through cunning or violence). Bonaventure makes a further distinction, essential in his analysis, which is based squarely upon the conventional view of authority. In examining the source of authority in problematic cases, one must distinguish between the perspective of the subject and that of the sovereign. The subject's perspective is framed by the conventional view:

---

[338]Liber II Sent. 44,2,1, Sed contra, d.

[339]Bonaventure's discussion does not formally distinguish the acquisition from the retention for purposes of his analysis. As we have seen, Aquinas does distinguish between the origin and the use of sovereignty. See II Scriptum super Libros Sent. 44,1, Solutio.

[340]Liber II Sent. 44,2,1, Respondeo.

[341]Ibid.

> In relation to the merit of the subject, such presidence [of wicked sovereigns] is just when it is either for the testing of the good subjects or for the punishment of the evil. . . . . And indeed the first way is said to be done and ordained by God, as is said: "He makes the hyprocrite to reign on account of the sins of the people," and again: "I gave them a king in my anger."[342]

From the perspective of the sovereign, however, some ambivalence remains. In Bonaventure's view, this sovereignty "is said to be with the permission of God, but not with his approval. . . ."[343] Accordingly, in the main Bonaventure is prepared to concede the truth of the position taken by the enumerated arguments which open the question. Like Aquinas, he accepts the fact that sovereignty in its essential capacity is always from God. Unlike Aquinas, however, he qualifies this view; it is always from God, but only from the conventional perspective of the subject. From the perspective of a given sovereign, a moral judgment must be made concerning the extent to which he justly acquired and maintained his sovereignty.

Thus, Bonaventure can turn aside the first argument of the Sed contra by reference to the distinction of the subject's perspective. Here he again emphasizes the conventional view. "For the civil power of evil persons is from an avenging God."[344] Aquinas, on the other hand, resolves an identical argument by stressing that here "the form of sovereignty itself is established by God."[345]

Similarly, with regard to the second argument, pointing out the unjust rule of many sovereigns, Bonaventure concedes the injustice, from the

---

[342]Ibid.

[343]Ibid.

[344]Ibid., ad 1.

[345]II Scriptum super Libros Sent. 44,1,2, ad 1.

perspective of our moral judgment of the sovereign, but validates the essential capacity of the sovereign as a "punishment of evildoers and for the praise of the good. . . ."[346] Again, Aquinas emphasizes that the problem is capable of resolution by reference to the form of sovereignty itself.

On the argument concerning the disorder of unjust rule, problematic since it appears to repudiate the notion that authority is essentially orderly, both commentators rely upon the conventional view as an explanation of this apparent inconsistency. Bonaventure, clearly committed to this view in principle, gives an extended discussion of the issue.[347] As we have already seen, for Aquinas this resolution is not wholly consistent with the basic approach taken in his Solutio, and his discussion here is somewhat perfunctory.[348]

In response to the empirical arguments pointing out that sovereigns are in fact overthrown, there is likewise some tension between the views of the two commentators. For Bonaventure, civil authority is never given absolutely or unconditionally, and so it is not inherently inconsistent that some sovereigns lose their power.[349]

Even in the case of usurped power, however, it may follow "the order of justice,"[350] and hence be from God. For Aquinas, on the other hand, these cases appear to be problematic. He tentatively relies upon the notion that this disorder may be from God "in punishment of those placed under [usurpers] deserve such a sovereign."[351]

---

[346]Liber II Sent. 44,2,1, ad 2, citing 1 Peter 2:14. Cf. Part III, note 54, infra.

[347]Liber II Sent. 44,2,1, ad 3.

[348]See II Scriptum super Libros Sent. 44,1,2, ad 5.

[349]Liber II Sent. 44,2,1, ad 5-6.

[350]Ibid., ad 6.

[351]II Scriptum super Libros Sent. 44,1,2, ad 3.

Bonaventure's response to the argument drawn from natural law may lead us to his second question under this article. Bonaventure distinguishes between "the universal dictate of nature [and] the natural dictate of some determined condition, in which there may indeed be no subjection to servitude nor authority of any power."[352] It is an examination of just such determined states or conditions which is carried out in the second question, which considers whether the power for governing is a natural institution or a punishment for sin. The parallel text in Aquinas' sentential commentary is the third article of the first question.

Bonaventure's discussion begins with a series of enumerated arguments to the effect that this power is a natural institution. The first argument relies upon a scriptural text, "Let us make man in our image and likeness and let him rule. . . ."[353] This authority is somewhat ambiguously employed, as the text of the argument itself notes.[354]

The second enumerated argument parallels the second paragraph of Aquinas' Sed contra on the same issue. Here Bonaventure presents the argument that, since one finds order and degrees among the angels, who are perfect in nature and grace, human order and degrees should not necessarily be incompatible with natural institutions. Likewise, the third enumerated argument parallels the first paragrpah of Aquinas' Sed contra. Here it is argued that civil authority may be viewed as a natural institution since it partakes essentially of nobility and dignity. If this is so, even in our corrupt state, then "so much more is it [fitting] to a natural institution."[355]

---

[352] Liber II Sent. 44,2,1, ad 4.

[353] Genesis 1:26.

[354] See Part III, text and accompanying notes 59-61, infra.

[355] Liber II Sent. 44,2,2,3.

The fourth amd final enumerated argument has no explicit parallel in Aquinas' <u>Sed contra</u>. The argument emphasizes the role of civil authority in conserving the natural order. It asserts that anything which serves such a purpose is necessarily a natural institution. In function, this purpose is not incompatible with the conventional view of civil authority itself. Indeed, the argument cites Augustine's <u>De civitate Dei</u> as authority, stating that the role of civil authority is demonstrated

> by what Augustine says: "Penal servitude is ordained by the law which commands that the natural order be preserved and forbids it to be disturbed." But the power for ruling and penal servitude are ordained for the same thing, and therefore the rest follows.[356]

The <u>Sed contra</u> argues for the position that civil authority is not a natural institution. There are several parallel arguments among those enumerated at the beginning of Aquinas' discussion in the third article, first question, of his commentary. Both begin with an argument based upon Gregory's statement that God made all men equal, but that a secret or hidden arrangement of God subordinated some men to others.[357] In the context of the present argument, both commentators take this dictum to mean that, but for the loss of the natural state or condition, there would have been equality among men.

Again, as to the second argument, the texts are parallel. What is noteworthy within Bonaventure's text is the fact that the argument in the <u>Sed contra</u> relies upon the text of Augustine cited in the

---

[356]<u>Ibid</u>., 44,2,2,4, quoting <u>De civitate Dei</u> 19:15.

[357]The commentators paraphrase the passage somewhat differently, but it does not appear that there is any material effect on the sense of the passage. Cf. Part II, text at note 26, infra, and Part III, text at note 64, infra.

previous series of arguments. Here the argument is that, in Augustine's view, only the irrational creatures, and not rational man, were intended by God to be ruled.[358]

In the third argument of the Sed contra the position is taken, relying on the Institutes,[359] that the civil power functions as an obstruction to natural freedom. Thus, it is not a feature of the natural condition of man. Aquinas relies rather upon Aristotle[360] for the proposition that civil power functions coercively, leading to the same conclusion.

Ultimately, the conventional view has millenial underpinnings. All unnatural limitations and coercion, including the impediments of civil authority, are to dissolve with the return of the believer to a natural state of grace. Relying upon another text of the De civitate Dei,[361] the final argument of the Sed contra asserts that

> in the glorification of men "faults will be removed and nature will be retained." But in the state of grace the civil power of authority and the subjection of servitude will not remain. Therefore, these do not appear to be in human nature with respect to what is ordained, but only with respect to what is failed or corrupted.[362]

---

[358]Of similar import is Liber II Sent. 44,2,2, Sed contra, d-e. See also II Scriptum super Libros Sent. 44,1,3,3.

[359]See Part III, text and accompanying note 66, infra.

[360]See Part II, text and accompanying note 30, infra.

[361]See De civitate Dei 22:17.

[362]Liber II Sent. 44,2,2, Sed contra, f. Cf. II Scriptum super Libros Sent. 44,1,3,5, citing 1 Corinthians 15:24.

Bonaventure's *Respondeo* depends upon a distinction between various determined conditions of man, "namely, the state of created nature, of fallen nature and nature glorified."[363] In the broadest sense, the power for ruling may refer to man's instrumental power over his possessions. This sort of power exists in each of the states. Of course, this sort of power is not at issue in the problem of civil authority.

A second sense of power, the "common" sense of the term, "is said to be the excellence of power in commanding that which is fit for reason and direction."[364] This sense, Bonaventure states, applies both to the state of created nature and that of the fallen state. However, this sense apparently does not apply to the millenial state of nature glorified.

A third sense of power, the "proper" sense, is the corecive power. This represents a restriction of freedom, and thus applies only to the state of fallen nature. "[I]t exists . . . as a punishment for sin, not as a natural institution."[365]

However, having made these distinctions, distinctions not dissimilar in any material respect from those found in Aquinas' sentential commentary, Bonaventure sets them to one side and stresses only the third, "proper" sense of the term. He writes:

> because we speak here of the power for ruling in that way, on that account the reasons shown are to be conceded, that such a power does not exist in man according to his primary condition or according to the state of created nature.[366]

---

[363]*Liber II Sent.* 44,2,2, *Respondeo*.

[364]Ibid.

[365]Ibid.

[366]Ibid.

Unlike Aquinas, therefore, Bonaventure presents an ambivalent attitude toward the status of civil authority. Essentially, the differences between the two commentators may appear to be one of emphasis. Aquinas, having arrived at a distinction between "guiding" and "dominating" modes of civil authority, is at pains to emphasize the natural character of the guiding mode. While Bonaventure's <u>Respondeo</u> provides similar distinctions, he lays particular stress upon the unnatural, coercive power. This for him is the primary connotation, the proper sense, of the term. As a result, he rejects the position taken by the enumerated arguments which opened the discussion.

He dismisses the first enumerated argument, based on scriptural texts, as referring only to the first and second senses of the term civil power. His response is much the same with respect to the ⁻rgument based upon the example of the hierarchy of the angels.

His attitude towards these arguments is not, however, simply a matter of distinguishing one sense from another. On the issue of the property of excellence to be found in civil authority, the basis of the third argument, he expressly repudiates the notion that there is any inherent excellence to be found there:

> although it may be a property of excellence in him who presides, still it is said to be an indignity to him who is subject. And thus by nature it can be appropriate for man with respect to the other inferior creatures, yet with respect to other men it is not appropriate by nature, but . . . in punishment of sin.[367]

Any hope that the ambivalence of Bonaventure's attitude might leave open some possibility of inherent, positive value in civil authority is decisively negated by his response to the fourth and

---

[367]<u>Ibid.</u>, 44,2,2, ad 3.

final enumerated argument. This argument, so closely paralleled in Aquinas' own discussion, asserts inherent value for civil authority in its role in the conservation of the natural order. Bonaventure's response is impassioned, emphatic and wholly negative:

> In accordance with the state of his first condition, [nature] dictates that man in fact is to be made equal to man. However, in accordance with the state of corruption, it dictates that man is to be subject to man and that man is to be a servant to man, so that the evil are repressed and the good are defended. . . . Nevertheless, it would not have been thus if man had remained in the state of innocence. . . .[368]

It would appear, therefore, that Bonaventure affirms the conventional view that civil authority is without inherent, positive value. To what extent, then, is there any necessity for subjection to the power for governing? This issue is the subject of Bonaventure's third article. The first question is whether Christians are required to subject themselves to secular authority. This discussion has its parallel in the second article, second question, of Aquinas' commentary.

Bonaventure's discussion begins with a series of enumerated arguments in support of the position that Christians are subject to this authority. The first argument quotes St. Peter's exhortation, "Servants, be submissive to your masters. . . ."[369] The same passage is cited by Aquinas in the first paragraph of his *Sed contra* in the parallel article.

The second and third arguments represent little more than a series of quoted texts from Romans 13:1-7, the central text of much medieval philosophical discussion of the problem of the duty owed to civil

---

[368] Ibid., 44,2,2, ad 4.

[369] 1 Peter 2:18, quoted in *Liber II Sent.* 44,3,1,1.

authorities. Again there is a parallel in Aquinas' Sed contra, which quotes Paul's dictum that "He who resists authority, resists the ordinance of God."[370]

The fourth enumerated argument, with no citation of authority, simply asserts that "to be subject to a man is not a fault or an evil, but to the contrary is meritorious."[371] This assertion may be viewed as an affirmation of the positive value of civil authority, but the argument remains somewhat ambiguous on this point.

Taken as a whole, it must be admitted, the series of arguments is perfunctory and detached. This fact is nowhere better illustrated than in the fifth argument, which actually states little more than the fact that "on this question there are many authorities which can be obtained like those from all the epistles of St. Paul."[372]

The arguments of the Sed contra are somewhat more animated. For the most part, these arguments reflect the attitude that acceptance of the faith should remove the believer from the purview of civil authorities. The enumerated arguments opening the second article, second question, of Aquinas' discussion parallel those of Bonaventure's Sed contra. In both cases, the first argument relies upon Christ's statement that "the children are free,"[373] interpreting "children" to refer to the believers themselves.

Both discussions stress the argument that acceptance of the faith frees man from servitude.[374] Both also assert the dissolution of lesser, legal

---

[370]Romans 13:2.

[371]Liber II Sent. 44,3,1,4.

[372]Ibid., 44,3,1,5. Of course, the perfunctory attitude here is somewhat similar to what finds in Lombard's text itself.

[373]Matthew 17:25.

[374]Cf. Liber II Sent. 44,3,1, Sed contra, b-c, and II Scriptum super Libros Sent. 44,2,2,2.

bonds as a result of the formation of the greater bond imposed by the acceptance of divine law.[375] However, there is no parallel in Bonaventure's <u>Sed contra</u> to the arguments in Aquinas' discussion with respect to the more problematic case of the duty of obedience due to the usurping tyrant.[376]

Bonaventure's <u>Respondeo</u> concentrates on the various senses in which man may be said to be subject to some form of servitude. Each sense may be seen as manifesting one aspect of the problem of the existence of evil and misery in the world. There is a servitude of sin, in which condition the sinner becomes a slave of sin. There is also a servitude of punishment and death. Finally, there is what Bonaventure calls a "servitude of condition," which is "the restriction of freedom by force, not so far as the internal movement of the will is concerned, . . . but so far as concerns the external."[377] There is, in Bonaventure's view, a causal relationship among these types of servitude. Reflecting the conventional view, he asserts that

> the servitude of punishment could not exist unless the servitude of fault were to precede it. Nor could the servitude of condition follow unless those both preceded.[378]

In accepting faith, one may be freed from the first servitude. The other servitudes remain a part of the corrupt condition of mankind. Hence, without affirming any inherent, positive value as a justification for subjection to civil authority, Bonaventure does insist that it must be endured.

---

[375]Cf. <u>Liber II Sent.</u> 44,3,1, <u>Sed contra</u>, d, and II <u>Scriptum super Libros Sent.</u> <u>44,2,2,3</u>. See also <u>Liber II Sent.</u> 44,3,1, <u>Sed contra</u>, e, citing Anselm, <u>Cur Deus Homo</u> 1:5, asserting that believers are servants of Christ alone.

[376]See II <u>Scriptum super Libros Sent.</u> 44,2,2,4-5.

[377]<u>Liber II Sent.</u> 44,3,1, <u>Respondeo</u>.

[378]<u>Ibid</u>.

Thus, in rejecting the position advocated by the arguments in the <u>Sed contra</u>, Bonaventure argues, first, that Christ's statement about the "children" being free is to be read as applying only to Christ and "his perfect imitators."[379]

Second, and more generally, while the faith frees man from the servitude of transgression or sin, the liber-ating nature of faith cannot in Bonaventure's view be invoked, as the <u>Sed contra</u> arguments would, to negate the necessity of subjection to the commands of civil authority. As Bonaventure has already emphasized in the <u>Respondeo</u> of the previous question, the ultimate liberating effect of faith is millenial in its perspective, looking to the state of nature glorified.[380] Thus, as Bonaventure states, "here freedom from guilt is begun, but there freedom from misery and from every human power is consummated."[381]

This portion of the commentary closes with the second question of the third article, which, as in the case of Aquinas' commentary, concerns the degree of obedience which the religious owes to his prelate. The discussion is specialized, and it does not materially advance our understanding of Bonaventure's resolution of the problem of civil authority.

In the third major portion of the commentary, Bonaventure presents a series of "Doubts concerning the Writings of the Master." The identification of problematic passages in Lombard's <u>Sentences</u> became an almost standard feature of sentential commen-

---

[379]<u>Liber II Sent</u>. 44,3,1, ad 1. Aquinas makes a similar argument. See II <u>Scriptum super Libros Sent</u>. 44,2,2, ad 1.

[380]This attitude is the historical view of the early period of the Church. See W. T. Jones, <u>A History of Western Philosophy</u>, 2nd ed. Vol. II: <u>The Medieval Mind</u> (New York: Harcourt Brace Jovanovich, Inc., 1969), pp. 116-20.

[381]<u>Liber II Sent</u>. 44,3,1, ad 5.

taries.[382] Brief discussion of this portion of the commentary has already been included in the previous discussion of Lombard's own text.[383] Of particular note here, however, is Bonaventure's brief consideration of the degrees of authority and the relationship between "superior" and "inferior" authorities. The discussion is prompted by Lombard's quotation of Augustine's reference to "the degrees of authority in human affairs."[384] The discussion loosely parallels Aquinas' more extended treatment of the same topic,[385] but it is by no means as detailed or formal. Two features of Bonaventure's discussion are to be noted. First, he makes the same distinction as Aquinas between: (i) an inferior authority whose power flows entirely from the superior; and, (ii) the relative superior and inferior authorities whose powers both flow from some third, ultimately superior authority.[386] In the first case, the duty owed by the subject to the superior authority always overreaches that owed to the inferior in any situation of apparent conflict between the two. In the second case, conflicts of authority can only be resolved with reference to the directive of the third ultimately superior authority.

The second feature to be noted here is that, unlike Aquinas, Bonaventure does not even so much as allude to the problem of the relationship between papal and imperial authority, between sacerdos and rex.

---

[382]See generally, Edward S. Synan, "Brother Thomas, the Master and the Masters," in St. Thomas Aquinas 1274-1974: Commemorative Studies, 2 vols. (Toronto: Pontifical Institute for Medieval Studies, 1974), 2:219-242.

[383]See text at notes 339-343, supra.

[384]See Part I, text at note 19, infra.

[385]Cf. text at notes 94-108, supra.

[386]Cf. Part II, text at notes 75-80, infra, and Part III, text at notes 125-27, infra.

The application of the comparative method to the sentential commentaries of Aquinas and Bonaventure should reveal the fundamental differences in their views on the problem of civil authority. Perhaps it is even more instructive to realize that they reach their materially distinct positions largely through the use of the same philosophical method and upon the basis of the analysis of many of the same sources and authorities.

Nowhere is this striking contrast in results, drawn from much the same raw data, more apparent than in their respective treatments of the question of the status of civil authority. As has been seen, the question serves as a test of the opposing conventional and natural views of civil authority. Aquinas appears to endorse the natural view clearly in his support of the position that civil authority is a natural institution, though he does qualify this view by confining his support to the "guiding" mode of authority.

For Bonaventure, the outcome of philosophical reflection is perhaps more ambivalent. Indeed, we have seen that he approximates Aquinas' distinction between the "guiding" and "dominating" modes of authority in his own discussion. It nevertheless seems clear that Bonaventure wll not attach to this distinction the significance which it enjoys in Aquinas' treatment. To the contrary, he appears to identify civil authority as an essentially coercive power, one of the indices of man's corrupted nature. Ultimately, then, it does not appear that civil authority has inherent, positive value for Bonaventure.

Thus, this study is in basic agreement with such commentators as Bede Jarrett, who have expressed the view that, for Bonaventure, civil authority has its fundamental justification in its role of constraining the evil.[387]

---

[387]See, e.g., B. Jarrett, Social Theories of the Middle Ages (Westminster: The New Book Shop, 1942), p. 10. A similar view is expressed in J. Zeiller, L'idee de l'Etat dans saint Thomas d'Aquin (Paris: Alcan, 1910), pp. 70, 123-5, passim.

To the contrary, one recent commentator has argued that in fact Bonaventure views man as a social creature, and that the role of civil authority is ultimately the conservation of right order.[388] While it may be true that Bonaventure endorses the notion that civil authority is orderly,[389] it is nevertheless also true that throughout his discussion of the power for governing in his second article, and in his discussion of the duty of obedience owed to secular authorities in the first question of his third article, his position is in all material respects consistent with the conventional view of civil authority.

Further, there is no indication in the sentential commentary as reviewed in this study that Bonaventure would base his justification of civil authority upon any notion of its inherent characteristic of order.[390] Likewise, reliance on the fact that Bonaventure does identify certain "kinds of authority which existed before the Fall"[391] of man from the state of created nature is misplaced. The fault manifested by this reliance is an insufficient appreciation of the ambivalence of Bonaventure's attitude towards those kinds of authority distinct from the coercive authority. In the final analysis, Bonaventure appears unconcerned with these other types of power. In stark contrast to Aquinas' view of civil authority as orderly and guiding, for Bonaventure it is the coercive power which fundamentally defines civil authority in his view.

---

[388]See De Benedictis, pp. 102, 189. In arguing for the proposition that Bonaventure endorses a view of man as a social creature, De Benedictis cites to the pastoral *Sermones de Tempore*, 1:9, as well as the *Collationes in Hexaemeron*, coll. 6. He gives no reference to the sentential commentary on this issue. The pastoral references are inconclusive on their own terms, and De Benedictis does not adequately address the direct, conflicting references in the sentential commentary.

[389]Cf., e.g., *Liber II Sent.* 44,2,1, ad 3.

[390]See ibid. (order in imposition of punishment).

[391]De Benedictis, p. 175.

PART I

SELECTION FROM THE *SENTENCES* OF PETER LOMBARD

PART I

SELECTION FROM THE SENTENCES OF PETER LOMBARD

Book Two, Distinction 44[1]

On the Potential for Sin: Whether it exists in Man or the Devil from God

Next something worthy of consideration presents itself, namely, whether the potential for sin[2] arises in us from God or from ourselves. Some hold that, whatever potential for acting rightly might arise in us from God, the potential for sin is certainly not from God, but from ourselves or from the devil, just as the morally bad will is not in us from God, but from ourselves and the devil, while the good is in us solely from God. On the other hand, the source of the morally good will and of knowledge is not produced in man of himself, but is provided and granted by divine influence. God has clearly revealed this in the following way. Neither the devil nor any of his angels have been nor will be able to regain the morally good will from which they were thrust into darkness. If after turning from God, it were possible for human nature to lose the goodness of the will and yet still possess it from itself, it would have been all the more possible for the angelic nature to do so. The latter is to such a greater extent provided with this faculty, as it is less burdened by the weight of an earthly body. Hence, neither man nor angel can possess the morally good will from himself, but only the bad. Similarly, concerning the potential for good and evil, others say (by way of

---

[1] This translation is based primarily upon the Latin text of Peter Lombard as it appears in the following works: Thomas Aquinas, Scriptum super Libros Sententiarum Magistri Petri Lombardi Episcopi Parisiensis, ed. R. P. Mandonnet, 4 vols. (Paris: P. Lethielleux, 1929), 2:1113-4. John Duns Scotus, Commentaria Oxoniensia ad IV Libros Magistri Sententiarum, ed. M. Fernandez Garcia, 2 vols. (Florence: Typographia Collegii S. Bonaventurae, 1914), 2:907-8.

[2] Potentia peccandi. Alternatively, this term may be rendered as "power to sin."

metaphor to the will) that the former comes from God, but not the latter.

Authorities affirm the Notion that the Potential for Sin is from God

However, it has been shown beyond doubt by the witness of many holy men that the power for evil[3] comes from God, from whom all power comes. For the Apostle says: "There is no authority[4] except from God,"[5] by which we should understand not only the power for good, but also for evil. Further, Christ says to Pilate, "You would have no power over me unless it had been given to you from above."[6] Certainly, as Augustine says,[7] the wickedness of men encompasses essentially[8] the desire to be harmful, but it does not have the power if he does not give it. For that reason, before he took any action against Job, the devil said to the Lord, "Put forth your hand,"[9] that is, "Give me the power," because the wicked have no power except from God. "Through me kings reign, and through me rulers[10] possess the earth."[11] Hence, Job says of the Lord, "He makes the hypocrite to reign on account of the sins of the people.[12] Of the people of Israel God says, "I gave them a king in my anger."[13] Certainly, the will for wickedness can come from the spirit of man. Yet

---

[3] Potestas mali.

[4] Potestas.

[5] Romans 13:1.

[6] John 19:11.

[7] In Psalm. 32:3.

[8] Per se.

[9] Job 2:5.

[10] Tyranni, i.e., "absolute rulers."

[11] Proverbs 8:15-16.

[12] Job 34:30.

[13] Hosea 13:11.

there is no power except from God, and this is a secret and fitting justice. Through the power given to the devil, God performs his own just deeds. Yet Gregory says of this, "The exaltation of pride, not the ordinance of power, is to be blamed. God granted the potential; the wickedness of our mind discovered the exaltation of that potential. Let us therefore remove what comes from us, because the depraved action, not the just potential, is to be condemned."[14] It is clearly shown by this authority and many others that there is no power for good or evil, whatever it is, except from the impartial God, even if the impartiality may be unknown to you.

Whether there may ever be Resistance to Authority

Here a question is asked which cannot be passed over in silence. For it was said above that no power for sin or wickedness comes to man or the devil except from God. However, the Apostle says, "He who resists authority[15] has resisted the ordinance of God."[16] If therefore the power for evil comes to the devil from the ordinance of God, it appears that this power is not to be resisted. But it is known that the Apostle was speaking of secular authority, evidently of the king, the prince[17] and the like, to whom there is to be no resistance in what God commands to be rendered to them, certainly in taxes and the like. If in fact some prince or the devil commanded something contrary to God, then that is to be resisted. Hence, Augustine says, considering when there may be resistance to authority, "If an authority commands what you ought not to do, here by all means reject the authority,[18] a greater power being feared. Direct your attention to the de-

---

[14] In Moralibus 26:26.

[15] Potestati.

[16] Romans 13:2.

[17] Principe, i.e., "the leader."

[18] Hic sane contemme potestatem. Contemne, imperative of contemno, was no doubt intended. Aquinas paraphrases the passage with contemne in his expositio. See Part II, note 75, infra.

grees of authority in human affairs. If what the procurator commands is contrary to the proconsul's orders,[19] should it be performed? On the other hand, if the procurator commands one thing, and the emperor another, can there be any doubt that, the one being contemned, the other is to be obeyed? Therefore, if the emperor commands something and God something else, the former having been discredited, God is to be submitted to."[20] Therefore, we may resist the authority of men or the devil if it suggests something contrary to God. In doing this, we do not resist the ordinance of God, but conform to it. For thus God ordained that we obey no authority in evil.

Until now we directed the entire attention of the mind to these thoughts and studies which pertain to the mystery of the word incarnate so that we may be able to say at least some little bit about ineffable matters, thanks to God's revelation.

---

[19] The procurator was the Roman official to whom was entrusted the administration of the fiscal revenues of an imperial province. The proconsul was the Roman official who acted as an imperial lieutenant to the province. "As it was impossible that [Augustus] could personally command the legions of so many distant frontiers, he was indulged by the senate . . . in the permission of devolving the execution of his great office on . . . lieutenants. In rank and authority these officers seemed not inferior to the ancient proconsuls; but their station was dependent and precarious." (Edward Gibbon, The Decline and Fall of the Roman Empire, ed. D. M. Low (New York: Harcourt, Brace and Company, 1960), p. 35.)

[20] Serm. 62:8.

PART II

EXCERPTS FROM THE COMMENTARY OF THOMAS AQUINAS

PART II

EXCERPTS FROM THE COMMENTARY OF THOMAS AQUINAS[1]

Commentary on the Second Book of the Sentences of Master Peter Lombard Distinction 44

Textual Analysis[2]

Having already said so much about sin, as to the act of sin, here [Lombard] considers the following issues concerning the potential[3] for sin. It is divided into two parts. {1115}[4] In the first part, he delimits the potential for sin. In the second, he continues into the following book, at the place where

---

[1]This translation is based upon the following text: Thomas Aquinas, *Scriptum super Libros Sententiarum Magistri Petri Lombardi Episcopi Parisiensis*, ed. R. P. Mandonnet, 4 vols. (Paris: P. Lethielleux, 1929), 2:1114-36.

[2]The original has *Divisio Textus*, i.e., "Division of the Text." See M.-D. Chenu, *Toward Understanding Saint Thomas*, trans. A.-M. Landry and D. Hughes (Chicago: Henry Regnery Company, 1964), p. 277. However, elsewhere Chenu translates the term as "analysis," contrasting it with the "summary literal exposition" (*expositio textus*). Ibid., p. 97.

[3]Aquinas uses several terms all of which may be approximately translated as "power." To indicate the respective shades of meaning, (i) *potentia* is translated as "potential" or "potentiality;" (ii) *potestas*, as either "power" or "authority" as the context requires; (iii) *praelatio*, as "authority" or "sovereignty" as the context requires; and, (iv) *dominium*, as "civil power," rather than "dominion," a term which has lost much of its specific intended meaning in modern parlance. (In medieval law, the term carried the meaning "property." See John B. Morrall, *Political Thought in Medieval Times* (New York: Harper Torchbooks, 1962), p. 87.)

[4]Bracketted numbers in the text refer to page numbers of the Mandonnet edition, note 1, supra.

he says: "Until now we directed the entire attention of the mind to these thoughts and studies which pertain to the mystery of the word incarnate." The first part is divided into two sections. In the first section he inquires whether the potential for sin comes from God. In the second, he considers the obedience which is owed to those who possess the potential for sovereignty[5] from God, at the place where he says: "Here a question is asked which cannot be passed over in silence." On the question of the potential for sin, he makes three points. First, he puts forward the question. Second, he relates certain opinions, at the place where he says: "Some hold that, whatever potential for acting rightly might arise in us from God, the potential for sin is certainly not from God, but from ourselves or the devil." Third, he determines the truth at the place where he says: "However, it has been shown beyond doubt by the witness of many holy men that the power for evil comes from God."

"Here a question is asked which cannot be passed over in silence." Here he inquires concerning the duty owed to those who possess authority from God. First, he sets forth the question. Second, he solves it, at the place where he says: "But it is known that the Apostle was speaking of secular authority."

* * *

First Question

This question is two-fold: first, concerning the potential for sin; second, concerning obedience.

With respect to the first, three points are considered: first, whether the potential for sin may be good, and from God; second, since in the service of authority, power may exist for the perpetration of many sins which would not be possible but for him who is in the state of authority, whether still all authority comes from God; third, whether sovereignty, or civil power, comes from God as the establishment of a natural institution[6] or as punishment of a corrupt nature.

---

[5]*Potentiam praelationis*.

[6]*In ordinationem naturae institutae*, i.e., literally, "for the setting in order of ordained nature."

First Article

Whether the potential for sin comes from God

To proceed to the first point:

1. It appears that the potential for sin does not come from God. For to be capable of sin, as Anselm says,[7] is neither freedom nor {1116} a part of freedom. But every natural potentiality which exists in us for the performance of human acts has as its object the free choice of the will.[8] Therefore, the potential for sin is not some natural potentiality in us. It is also established that it is not a potentiality of grace, because nothing is ordained for sin through grace. Therefore, since every potentiality which is in us from God is of grace or of nature, it appears that the potential for sin does not arise in us from God.

2. Further, "The works of God are perfect."[9] Therefore, the more perfect something is, the more it ought to be reckoned among the divine works. But the act is more perfect than the potential. Since, therefore, the act of sin is not from God, neither will the potential for sin be from God.

3. Further, in human activity there comes together potentiality, knowledge and will. But the will for sin is not from God. Therefore, by the same reasoning, neither is the potential for sin.

4. Further, from an essential cause an effect is produced in accordance with a similarity to its cause. Hence from God, the essential cause of all things, all things are produced by retaining[10] his likeness as far as they can. This is so because from the first being come beings, and from the first living being, living beings. But in the potential for sin the creatures are not assimilated to God. Therefore, the potential for sin does not arise in us from God.

---

[7]*De lib. arbitrio* 1:1.

[8]*Ad liberum arbitrium pertinet*.

[9]Deuteronomy 32:4.

[10]*Retinentia*

5. Further, anything the use of which is evil, is itself evil, as Boethius says.[11] But the use of the potential for sin is sin itself, which is evil. But nothing which is evil comes from God. Therefore, the potential for sin is not from God.

But to the contrary, the Philosopher says[12] that rational powers[13] are of opposites. Therefore, there is likewise a potential for sin and a potential for acting rightly. But the potential for good is operative from God, thus also the potential for sin.

Further, every being comes from God. But the potential for sin is a certain kind of being. Therefore, the potential for sin is from God.

Solution

I respond by saying that a potentiality is known through its act. From a consideration of the act of sin, a judgment {1117} is to be made concerning the potential for sin. However, there are two features to the act of sin, namely, the substance of the act and the deformity or defect of the due circumstances. Hence, one should attend to these two things in the potential for sin itself. First, there is the potential itself, which is the principle of action. It is likewise the principle of both action regulated by reason and that which is not,[14] and this is from God. Second, a certain defect in it is to be considered according to which it may be capable of producing the deficient act. For the most perfect potentialities

---

[11]De diff. Topic. 2:2.

[12]The Mandonnet edition gives Metaphysics, Book 9, ch. 3 and 10, as the reference, but it would appear that ch. 3 and 9 are alluded to here.

[13]Potentiae rationales, i.e., powers under the influence of reason. Aquinas' terms potentia rationalis and potentia irrationalis are a translation of the Aristotelian expression, dynamis meta logou kai dynamis alogos. See Metaphysics, Book 9, ch. 2, 1046^{b}2. See also Roy J. Deferrari, A Latin-English Dictionary of St. Thomas Aquinas (Boston: St. Paul Editions, 1960), p. 809.

[14]Actus ordinati et inordinati.

never fall short of what they are ordained to be, as is evident in necessary beings. Hence it follows from the fact that a potential is impeded or held back from that to which it is naturally ordained that this arises from its defect, so far as it will yield to another cause which impedes it. Hence, since the potential of the human will is essentially ordained towards the good, it is necessarily the case that a failing from the good in its act is caused by some failing in itself. It is through that that it can be subdued by something, either by a pleasure, or suggestion, or something else. In this way it is drawn from what is natural for itself towards what is unnatural. Here, however, the defect exists according to what is from nothing. Moreover, as Avicenna proves, God is not directly the cause of such a defect, which is evidently a creature of nothing, because what conforms to a thing according to itself is not caused in it by another. Moreover, if abandoned to itself, a created thing is nothing. Hence, what is being from nothing is not the creature's from God, though the being of the creature is from God. For all that, it may be said that that defect is indirectly from God, though not as from a certain agent, but from a non-agent, that is, insofar as he himself does not provide this to the creature, as it is not from nothing. Thus he is said to be the cause of the privation of grace, which is a punishment, unless a creature be found not to be capable of this sort of perfection. That is to say, it may not come from nothing. For that reason, this defect is by no means from God, neither directly nor indirectly. Thus the potential for sin, so far as to what is of the potential is from God, but so far as the defect which is involved, the potential is not from God.

I therefore respond to the first point by saying that what is said to be capable of sin is not part of freedom, because it is not required for freedom of the will that it be capable of sin. However, it suffices for the concept of freedom[15] that it be capable of each of the contradictories. Still in these which are capable of sin, a sin may be committed through the free choice of the will, since the will is that by which a sin is committed and by which one lives properly, as Augustine says.[16]

---

[15] Ad rationem libertatis.

[16] 1 Retract. 9:4.

To the second point I respond that the act is always more perfect than the potential, by a perfection of its proper genus. Hence, a good act is more perfect in goodness that the good potential. Similarly, the bad act is more perfect in wickedness than the bad potential, {1118} since in the bad act there is evil absolutely, while in the potential for evil there is evil with qualifications. Therefore, the act which is bad is not said to be from God without qualification, but with qualifications. On the other hand, the potential for evil is said to be from God without qualification, and in a certain respect not to be from God. For perfection in wickedness is not perfection properly and absolutely speaking, but as it were, metaphorically, as we say "a perfect bandit" and the "perfection of blindness," as is said by Aristotle.[17]

To the third point I respond that the will can be taken in two ways: either as the potential of the will itself, or as its act. In the first way, the will by which a sin is committed is from God, while in the second way it is not. On the other hand, the potentiality never gives its name to the act, but the use of the potentiality itself is the sin. Therefore, the objection is based upon an equivocation of the term "will."

To the fourth point I respond that a certain good is perfect and a certain other imperfect. If therefore some name is given without imperfection to the goodness in us which comes from God, in accordance with which we are similar to him, it will be found to fit God and us, for example, wisdom, goodness and the like. However, the potential for sin names a good with imperfection, and therefore cannot fit God in whom nothing is imperfect.

To the fifth point I respond that the use of a thing is said to be that to which a thing is principally directed. However, the potentiality by means of which we are able to sin is not principally directed to evil but to good. Thus, to sin is not its use. Hence it does not follow that, if sin is evil, the potentiality is evil. Rather, it is good, since to depart from that which is good is evil.

---

[17]*Metaphysics*, Book 5, ch. 21.

Second Article

Whether all sovereignty comes from God

To proceed to the second point:

1. It appears that not all sovereignty comes from God. This is apparent from what is said in the passage: "They have set up kings, but not by me."[18]

2. Further, whatever is done perversely is not from God. However, some sovereignties are acquired perversely, as is the case in simony and in other things of that kind. Therefore, not all sovereignty is from God.

3. Further, sovereignty granted by the highest king cannot be usurped. Yet Boethius says[19] {1119} that the evil possess usurped power. Therefore, their sovereignty is not from God.

4. Further, what God gave, man ought not make away with, just as "What God has joined together, man may not separate."[20] Yet the authority of sovereignty is justly taken from certain persons. Therefore, their sovereignties are not from God.

5. Further, everything that is from God is ordained.[21] Yet in certain sovereignties there seems to be a great disorder, to the extent that the foolish is preferred to the wise, the child to the elder, the sinner to the just, as commonly happens. Therefore, not every sovereignty is from God.

But to the contrary, while it appears that the sovereignty of the good comes from God to a greater extent than that of the evil, still the sovereignties of the evil are from God: "He makes the hypocrite to

---

[18] Hosea 8:4.

[19] De consolatione philosophiae, Book 3.

[20] Matthew 19:6.

[21] The reference is probably to Romans 13:1.

reign on account of the sins of the people."[22] Therefore, all sovereignties are from God.

Further, everything which is ordered is from God, since from this very fact it is good. Yet in every sovereignty a certain order of the superior to the inferior is discovered. Therefore, every sovereignty is from God.

Solution

I respond by saying that, since God is said to be the author of good and not the author of evil, it is proper that, if in sovereignties some good and some evil is discovered, that sovereignty comes from God to the extent of the good which is in it. Yet to the extent of the evil which it imparts to itself, that does not come from God. Moreover, in sovereignty there are three features to consider, namely, the origin[23] of sovereignty, the mode, and the use. Accordingly, in certain cases, any one of these who attain sovereignty properly and exercise the act of sovereignty properly is good. But in fact, in certain cases the origin is bad, but the use is good, as in the case of one who does not attain sovereignty worthily, either because of their inadequacy or because of their mode of attaining it. Though they have acquired as undutifully as possible the act of sovereignty, they exercise it in a dutiful way. But in fact, in certain cases the reverse is true. On the other hand, the mode, or form, of sovereignty is good in all cases. For it consists in a certain order of the one as ruling and the other as being subject to. And since the judgment concerning a thing is to be given absolutely from a consideration of what it is formally in itself, accordingly it must be stated absolutely that every sovereignty is from God. But relatively to something, some sovereignties are not from God because their abuse is, of course, not from God, or yet because the unjust action through which one attains sovereignty is not from God. {1120}

---

[22] Job 34:30.

[23] The original has _principium_. An alternative translation, more often encountered, would be "priniciple," but the context of the _solutio_ makes "origin" an equally acceptable (and, in fact, more literal) translation.

I therefore respond to the first point by saying that the kings of the Jews are said to reign not from God insofar as, though Samuel argued against it, they wished to elect a king for themselves. But for all that, the form of sovereignty itself is established by God.

To the second point I respond that it is not unfitting that an effect comes from God, since for all that the unjust action, the effect of which it is, nevertheless does not come from God. How this happens is stated above. Similarly, it is not unfitting that sovereignty, insofar as its form is concerned, comes from God, although the unjust action through which one attains sovereignty does not come from God, except perhaps permissively.

To the third point I respond that the evil are said to possess usurped power insofar as they attain it undutifully. So far is it from them, since they are unworthy to be preferred to such distinguished individuals, although perhaps it happens that those who are injured by them might be deserving of the injury. And it follows from this that their sovereignty is from God in punishment of those placed under them who deserve such a sovereign.

To the fourth point I respond that, because of abuse, one may deprive oneself of a welcome privilege. Hence, even if they attained sovereignty from God, still it is fitting that the power of sovereignty is removed from them since they abused it. And each is from God, namely, both the fact that they had sovereignty, and the fact that they lost it justly. Of course, all life comes from God, yet some are deprived of life justly.

To the fifth point I respond that it is not entirely without order that unworthy men are chosen for sovereignties. For it is ordained in punishment of the subjects who merit this. "He makes the hypocrite to reign because of the sins of the people."[24] And again: "I gave them a king in my anger."[25] Whence it follows that, if every punishment comes from God, then such sovereignties are from God.

---

[24] Job 34:30.

[25] Hosea 13:11.

Third Article

Whether in the state of innocence there was a civil power

To proceed to the third point:

1. It appears that in the state of pure innocence, there would have been no sovereignty or civil power. For Gregory says,[26] "Nature made all men equal, but the hidden yet just arrangement of God subordinated some to others according to their merits." But if {1121} men had not sinned they would have retained the state of nature. Therefore, all would have been equal, and there would have been no sovereignty over them.

2. Further, Augustine says[27] that man made in the image of God is only placed over the irrational animals. But man is not compared to the animals except because of sin: "Man did not know when he was in honor; he is compared to the insensible beasts of burden and is made like them."[28] Therefore, if there had not been sin, there would not have been one man placed over another.

3. Further, civil power without a subject is not possible. But Augustine, in the passage cited above, and other holy men generally say that subjection is introduced in return for sin. And therefore civil power, or sovereignty, did not exist before there was sin.

4. Further, the Apostle says,[29] "The law is not laid down for the just man." But the Philosopher says[30] that the necessity for establishing kings and

---

[26] In Moralibus 21:15.

[27] De civitate Dei 19:15.

[28] The original cites Psalms 48:13, but the text appears to be a paraphrase of what is now known as Psalms 49:12 and 49:20.

[29] 1 Timothy 1:9.

[30] Nicomachean Ethics, Book 10, ch. 9, $1179^b 4$-18.

other princes was to write laws having a coercive force for acts of virtue which the more persuasive discourse of wise men did not possess. Therefore, if all men had complied with the justice in which they were established, there would not have been sovereignty.

5. Further, those things which follow pure nature still continue in heaven. But in the future every sovereignty will cease.[31] And therefore, in pure nature there would not have been any sovereignty.

But to the contrary, whatever is of merit would have been all the more noble in pure nature. But civil power and sovereignty have worthiness as their object. Therefore, they would have existed more fully by far in the state of pure nature.

Further, the state of pure nature was not higher than the state of the angels is now. But among the angels there is one order which is called dominations, and still others pertaining to sovereignty, such as principalities, powers and archangels.[32] And therefore in the state of human nature before sin there would have been sovereignty.

Solution

I respond by saying that the mode of sovereignty is two-fold, one ordained for guiding, the other, how-

---

[31]See 1 Corinthians 15:24.

[32]Dominations (or dominions), prinicipalities, powers and archangels, the names or four of the nine hierarchical orders of the angels, more or less connote degrees of "sovereignty." Indeed, that there is thought to be a hierarchical order of the angels at all would serve the force of the argument in the text. Historically, there had been disputes concerning the relative positions of the orders in the hierarchy, particularly between Dionysius the Areopagite (see his On Celestial Hierarchy) and Gregory the Great (in his Homilies on the Gospel). Aquinas discusses the orders in the Summa contra Gentiles, and he compares Dionysius and Gregory in the Summa Theologiae, I, Q. 108. Dante alludes to this controversy in Il Paradiso, lines 130-5. See also D. L. Sayers, trans., The Divine Comedy of Dante, 3 vols. (Harmondsworth: Penguin Books, Ltd., 1976), vol. 3: Paradise, p. 308.

ever, for dominating. Thus, the sovereignty of the master in relation to the slave is, as the Philosopher says,[33] that of the absolute ruler to the subject. However, the absolute ruler differs from the king, as the Philosopher says in the same place, because the king arranges his sovereignty for the good of the nation over which he presides, promulgating statutes and laws because of their usefulness to the nation. However, the absolute ruler establishes his sovereignty for his own advantage. On that account, the double mode of sovereignty aforementioned {1122} differs in this respect, because in the first case it is directed to the good of the subjects, in the second to the particular good of the ruler. Therefore, the second mode of sovereignty would not be possible in a state of pure nature, except with respect to those things which are ordained for man just as for an end. However, these are irrational creatures over all of whom man would preside for his convenience more fully by far than now. But the rational creature, so far as concerns himself, is not ordained as an end for another, as a man for another man. However, if this does occur, it will not be so, except insofar as man is likened to irrational creatures because of sin. Hence it is that the Philosopher, in the same place, likens the slave to an instrument, saying that the slave is an animate instrument and the instrument an inanimate slave. And on that account, such a sovereignty of man over man did not exist before sin. But the first sovereignty, which was established for the advantage of the subjects, did exist then with respect to some needs, though not for all. For there is a sovereignty for directing subjects in those things which are to be done and for completing their failings, so that the people are defended by kings, and again, for reforming customs, while the evil are punished and are forcibly led to acts of virtue. But since before sin there was nothing that could be harmful to man, neither indeed did the will of anyone gainsay the good. On that account, so far as concerns the last two mentioned needs, there was no sovereignty in the state of innocence. But so far as the first need only, namely, that which is for guidance in action or knowledge, it follows that one greater than another was endowed with the employment of wisdom and with the light of the intellect.

I therefore respond to the first point by saying

---

[33]*Nicomachean Ethics*, Book 8, ch. 10.

that by nature all were made equal in freedom, but not in natural perfections. For the free, according to the Philosopher,[34] is that which exists for the sake of itself.[35] Still, one man is not thus established as an end for another. On that account the second mode of sovereignty did not exist which took away the freedom of the subject. But the first mode, which brings no prejudice to freedom, was possible, since the subjects were not ordained for the good of the commander, but on the contrary, the guidance of the commander for the good of the subjects.

To the second point I respond that Augustine speaks with respect to the second mode of sovereignty. {1123}

And similarly to the third point.

To the fourth point I respond that, with respect to the necessity of writing laws with coercive force, there was no sovereignty, but there was with respect to other needs, as has been said.

To the fifth point I respond that I have already explained in Distinction Eleven how it is to be understood that every sovereignty is to be eliminated in the future. Nevertheless, if it is understood absolutely to be removed in the future, it does not follow that there was no sovereignty in the state of innocence, as that state was hitherto a state along the way. And along the way, that sovereignty through which one is guided by another is necessary, though it does not appear necessary to such an extent at the end of the way.

Second Question

Next a question is asked concerning obedience to sovereigns. And with respect to this three things are asked. First, whether obedience is a virtue, and if it

---

[34] The Latin text gives *Metaphysics*, Book 1, ch. 3, which is inapposite. Cf. the discussion of the nature of the slave in *Politics*, Book 1, ch. 4.

[35] *Quod sui causa est.*

is a virtue, whether it is a particular virtue.[36] Second, whether Christians are required to obey secular authorities, and particularly absolute rulers. Third, whether the religious[37] are required to obey their prelates in all things.

First Article

**Whether obedience
is a virtue**

To proceed to the first point:

1. It appears that obedience is not a virtue. For every virtue is the mean of two vices as the Philosopher says.[38] But obedience is not of this sort, because it is not corrupted through abundance, but is perfected if someone obeys in matters in which he he is not required to obey. Therefore, obedience is not a virtue.

2. Further, obedience depends upon a command. But a command extends itself to all acts of virtue, because they are all under the command of the law. Therefore, obedience is not a specific virtue[39] but follows from every virtue. That can be inferred from the definition given by Ambrose,[40] who says that sin is "a transgression of the law of God and a disobedience of heavenly commands."

3. Further, if obedience is a specific virtue, it

---

[36] *Virtus specialis.*

[37] The original has *profitentes obedientiam*. Alternatively, the discussion of this point in the text of the Third Article itself speaks of *religiosi professi*. In any event, the question is one of the specific obedience due from a religious to his spiritual "sovereign," the prelate, this question being a more technical or specialized variation of the Second Article.

[38] *Nicomachean Ethics*, Book 2, ch. 6.

[39] *Virtus determinata.*

[40] Ambrose's definition is discussed in Distinction Thirty-five.

is either one of the cardinal virtues or one of the collateral virtues. But it is not one of the cardinal virtues, because those are only four in number, among which obedience is not enumerated. {1124} Similarly, it is not found among the collateral virtues, as is clear if the collateral virtues are considered those which the Philosopher enumerates.[41]

4. If it is said that obedience is reduced to justice, then to the contrary, it could be argued that no virtue is perfected by the diminution of the concept of its object. This is evident in magnanimity, which looks to "the great" [i.e., magnum]. The greater that which is to be done is, the more it pertains to magnanimity. But justice looks to a debt or obligation as an object, because the act of justice consists in restoring to the other what is his. Since obedience is made perfect by the fact that the obligation is diminished, the less someone considers it, as Bernard says,[42] the more perfect is obedience. Therefore, it appears that obedience is not reduced to justice.

5. Further, justice is said to be legal in accordance with which man is made equal to its commands. But obedience looks to commands. Therefore, obedience is the same as legal justice. But legal justice, as the Philosopher says,[43] is all virtue. Therefore, obedience is not some specific virtue, but a general one.

6. Further, as Gregory says,[44] obedience is not so much a virtue as the mother of all virtues. But to be the mother of all virtues is fitting for charity. Therefore, obedience appears to be the same as charity, and thus it does not seem to be distinct from the other virtues.

But to the contrary, Hugh of Saint Victor says,[45] "Obedience is the virtue which embraces all enjoined

---

[41]See, e.g., Nicomachean Ethics, Book 4.

[42]De praec. et dispens. 7:16.

[43]Nicomachean Ethics, Book 5, ch. 1.

[44]In Moralibus, Book 35, ch. 14.

[45]Serm., ch. 16.

things, fulfilling necessity, unless the governing authority shall have stood in the way," and thus it is a particular virtue since a special act is assigned to it.

Further, the fact that something is ascribed to be the greatest in any type is something specific in that type. But Gregory says that obedience is the greatest of virtues. Therefore, obedience is a kind of specific virtue.

Solution

I respond by saying that obedience is a virtue, and a particular one. For, since dispositions, potentialities and acts are distinguished by their objects, it is appropriate that a virtue which has a specific object be considered a specific virtue. Moreover, an object is said to be specific by a specific concept, although that specific concept can be placed among many things or all things. For it appears that the same thing is often an object for different potentialities, {1125} thus color for vision, imagination and intellect, but under a different concept. Whence it happens that one specific virtue extends itself to acts of all virtues according to a specific concept. Thus the Philosopher says,[46] concerning magnanimity, that the great [magna] works in the acts of all virtues, and hence is a certain adornment of all other virtues. Such virtues are said to be general in a certain way, because they have a general matter, although they do have a specific object on account of the specific concept of the object which is discovered in many materials. And I say that in this way obedience is a specific virtue, because it directs attention to a specific concept, namely, of harmonizing command with obligation. And because to restore to another what is his and is owed to him is of justice, on that account obedience is a certain part of justice, and especially of divine justice. That is so because this "his" which is restored to the superiors (that is, the fulfillment of orders) is a certain part of such common property as is said to be owed, or which is "his," and indeed which can be demanded in the presence of the judge. For with respect to such things, justice is in a proper sense specific. But still, it is known that specific justice is taken in

---

[46]Citing Nicomachean Ethics, Book 4, ch. 8.

two ways, privately and publicly. As the Philosopher says,[47] specific justice, taken in its most private instance, is such only between those who possess a certain equality for that which they may stand in the presence of the prince, before whom one may claim from another what is his. According to this mode, justice is said to exist neither of the master for the slave, nor the father for the son, because those things which are the slave's are the master's, and those which are the son's are the father's. Generally, however, specific justice is still directed to the fact that a master restores to a slave what is his, or conversely, and thus concerning the others, because according to this mode, the aforementioned equality is not required. And by means of this mode of conceiving specific justice, obedience pertains to justice, because in obedience the inferior restores to the superior what he owes.

I therefore respond to the first point by saying that obedience, like the other virtues, can be the median of two vices. However, it must be known that an overabundance as to any circumstance at all cannot be grasped in all virtues, other circumstances being properly ordained, as is evident in that virtue which is called truth, the median of which is directed to the fact that a man shows himself to be what he is. However, its excess is not related to an excess in terms of quantity ("how much"), other circumstances being properly ordained, as if one could serve this virtue excessively, but it is that someone makes more of {1126} himself than circumstances warrant, in terms of its essence ("what"). Similarly, I also say that an excess of obedience is grasped where one obeys in those things in which one ought not to obey, not however with respect to what one may obey more than one ought, other ordained circumstances being supposed.

To the second point I respond that even if obedience extends itself to all acts of virtue, it still does not consider in those things what is peculiar to each virtue. For it does not elicit the act of fortitude insofar as it is the median between fear and audacity, but it considers in all acts of virtue one particular concept, namely, the duty to be performed because of the command of the superior.

---

[47]*Nicomachean Ethics*, Book 5, ch. 6.

To the third point I respond that obedience is reduced to specific justice. But it is known that one virtue is reduced to another in two ways: either as a part of it, or as an adjunct to it. As a part, virtue reduces to virtue, whatever is reduced having for an object part of the object of that virtue to which it is reduced. For example, the object of temperature is the pleasant with respect to touch, a certain part of which is the sexually pleasant, and another is the pleasant in foods. Thus, chastity is reduced to temperance as a part of it, and similarly sobriety, the object of which is the pleasant in foods. And in this way obedience is reduced to specific justice, as is evident from what has been said. But as an adjunct, it is reduced when the virtue to which it is reduced has for an object that which is the principal thing in some other material. That which is reduced, which is said to be an adjunct, has for an object that which is less principal. In this way gentleness is reduced to fortitude, because the object of fortitude is in the greatest troubles, which are concerned with death, as wars are. But gentleness has for an object the remaining troubles, which are provocations of anger, in which gentleness comprises the median. And in this way modesty, which serves as the median in the pleasures of the other senses, and good nature or equanimity,[48] which serves as the median in the pleasures of games, are reduced to temperance.

To the fourth point I respond that the perfection of any virtue can be attended to in two ways: either as what is peculiar to itself, or as what is peculiar to a superior virtue, which orders its acts to be done. I say therefore that the perfection of obedience is not derived from the diminution of duty, as to the particular concept of obedience, but as to the particular concept {1127} of charity, which thus orders its acts to be done, and the acts of the other virtues.

To the fifth point I respond that obedience is not the same as legal justice. For legal justice looks to the command of the law, and the acts of virtue which are ordained by the law, insofar as they involve another, as the Philosopher says,[49] that is, insofar as

---

[48] *Eutrapelia*, i.e., the capacity for or virtue of good or agreeable teasing or joking.

[49] *Nicomachean Ethics*, Book 5, ch. 1.

the acts of virtue commanded by law are ordained for the good of the state, which is ruled by laws. But obedience looks solely to the command so far as it has the nature of an obligation, from the ordering of itself to a superior. Hence, it is not necessary that it be a general virtue.

To the sixth point I respond that one virtue can arise from another in two ways. Either it arises by way of a final cause, and in this way a virtue is said to arise from another so far as its act is ordained for the end of another virtue. Thus charity, the object of which is the ultimate end, is said to be the mother of all virtues. Or it arises in another way, according to which another virtue is either caused or maintained by the acts of one virtue. And thus obedience is said to be the mother of virtues, because the commands of superiors are ordained for this, so that they lead to virtues by admonishing acts of virtues themselves, which cause political virtues, leading to custom, but they facilitate the acquired virtues. Nor do I call an act of virtue only what comes from a virtue, but also what is either thus facilitating a virtue or causing it. Thus, a person existing in mortal sin can exercise an act of obedience, although he is without obedience and the other virtues.

Second Article

Whether Christians are required to obey secular authorities, and especially absolute rulers

To proceed to the second point:

1. It appears that Christians are not required to obey secular authorities, and particularly absolute rulers. It is said, "Therefore the children are free."[50] For if in any kingdom at all the children of that king, who is placed over that kingdom, are free, then the children of the king to whom all kingdoms are subordinated ought to be free in any such kingdoms. But Christians have become sons of God: "Indeed the Spirit gives testimony to our spirit that we are children of God."[51] Therefore, they are free everywhere, and they are not required to obey secular authorities.

---

[50]Matthew 17:25.

[51]Romans 8:16.

{1128}

2. Further, slavery was introduced because of sin. . . . But through baptism men are cleansed of sin. Therefore they were freed from slavery, and the same conclusion follows as before.

3. Further, a greater bond dissolves a lesser one, as a new law dissolves observance of an old law. But in baptism man is obligated to God, which obligation is greater than that by which man is obligated to another through slavery. Therefore, through baptism he is absolved of slavery.

4. Further, anyone is allowed to regain what has been unjustly taken from him, if the opportunity offers itself. But many princes usurped the dominions of their lands tyrannically. Therefore, as the power for rebelling against them is conceded, men are not required to obey these princes.

5. Further, no one is required to obey him whom it is permissible, even laudable, to slay. But Tullius[52] justifies those who killed Julius Caesar, though a friend and relative, because, like an absolute ruler, he had usurped the rights of empire.[53] Therefore, no one is required to obey such people.

But to the contrary, "Servants, be submissive to your masters with all respect."[54]

Further, "He who resists authority, resists the ordinance of God."[55] But to resist the ordinance of God is not permitted. Therefore, neither is resistance of secular authority permitted.

Solution

I respond by saying that, as has been said, obedience looks to the obligation of observing in the com-

---

[52] I.e., Marcus Tullius Cicero.

[53] De Officiis, Book 1, section 26.

[54] 1 Peter 2:18. The Latin text has "XI" instead of "2."

[55] Romans 13:2.

mand which is served. However, this duty is caused by the order of a sovereignty which possesses constraining force,[56] not only temporally but also spiritually as a matter of conscience, as the Apostle says,[57] insofar as the order of sovereignty derives from God, as the Apostle indicates in the same place. And thus, insofar as what comes from God, the Christian is required to obey such people, but not insofar as a sovereignty which is not from God. Still, it has been said that sovereignty can fail to be from God in two ways: either as to the mode of acquiring sovereignty, or as to the abuse of sovereignty. As to the first, it happens in two ways: either because of a defect in the person (because he is unworthy), or because of a defect in the mode of acquisition itself (namely, because he acquired sovereignty through violence, or through simony, or by some other illicit method). From the first defect, he is not impeded from acquiring the right of sovereignty, and since sovereignty with respect to {1129} its form is always from God, and this creates the duty of obedience, the subjects are thus required to obey such superiors, though they may be unworthy. But the second defect impedes the right to sovereignty. For he who usurps civil power through violence does not truly become a sovereign or master. Thus, if the opportunity offers itself, anyone can cast off such civil power, unless it so happens afterwards that he becomes a true master, either through the consent of the subjects or through the authority of superiors. However, there can be an abuse of sovereignty in two ways. Either, in the first case, what is commanded by a sovereign is contrary to that for which the sovereignty is established, as if it commands an act of sin contrary to virtue, for the protection and preservation of which the sovereignty is established. In that case, one is not only not required to obey, one is even required not to obey, as the holy martyrs suffered death rather than obey the impious commands of the absolute rulers. Or, in the second case, he compels that to which the order of sovereignty does not extend itself, as if the master demands tribute which the servant is not required to give, or in other similar cases. In that case, the subject is not required to obey, nor indeed is he required not to obey.

---

[56] <u>Virtutem coactivem</u>.

[57] The reference is probably to Romans 13:3-6.

I therefore respond to the first point by saying that that sovereignty which is established for the benefit of the subjects does not abolish the freedom of the subjects. And thus it is not unsuitable that those who have become children of God through the Holy Spirit are subject to such sovereignty. Or, I respond that Christ is speaking of himself and his disciples, who neither were in a servile condition, nor had temporal goods by which they were obliged to pay tribute to their masters. And thus, it does not follow that every Christian participates in this kind of freedom, but only those who follow the apostolic life, possessing nothing in this world and being immune from the servile condition.

To the second point I respond that baptism does not immediately put an end to all penalties following from the sin of the first parents (like the inevitability of death and blindness and other things of that kind), but regenerates in living hope of that life in which all of those penalties are abolished. And thus, it does not follow that someone who is baptized is immediately freed from the servile condition, though that is a punishment for sin.

To the third point I respond that the greater bond does not dissolve the lesser, unless they are mutually incompatible. Since there cannot be semblance and truth at the same time, accordingly, by the coming of the truth of the Gospel, the semblance of the old law ceases. {1130} But the bond by which one is bound in baptism is compatible with the bond of servitude, and thus it is not dissolved by the former.

To the fourth point I respond that those who attain authority through violence are not true rulers. Hence, neither are the subjects required to obey them except as was said before.

To the fifth point I respond that Tullius speaks to the case where someone usurps civil power through violence, the subjects being unwilling or even forced to consent, and where there is no recourse to a superior authority through whom judgment can be made concerning the usurpation. For then he who kills the absolute ruler for the liberation of the country is praised and obtains reward.

Third Article

Whether the religious[58] are required to obey their prelates in all things

To proceed to the third point:

1. It appears that those who vow obedience are required absolutely to obey their prelates. "Children, obey your parents in all things."[59] But one is required to obey a spiritual father more than a carnal one. Therefore, spiritual children, particularly those who vow obedience, are required to obey their spiritual fathers in all things.

2. Further, Benedict says[60] that even if the prelate ordered the impossible, nevertheless the impossible should be attempted. But much more is required for obedience in possible things than in impossible ones. Therefore, one who vows obedience is absolutely required to obey the prelate in all possible things.

3. Further, any religious order principally has three essential vows, namely, chastity, poverty and obedience. But one is required to observe chastity in all ways, and similarly poverty, since one may not possess anything of one's own. And therefore, one is required to observe obedience thus, to obey absolutely in all things.

4. Further, judgment concerning a superior is not left to an inferior. But if the subject had to determine in which matters he was to obey and in which not, judgment concerning the command of the superior would be left to the subject himself. Therefore, the subject is absolutely required to obey in all things.

5. Further, any Christian is required to obey the spiritual prelates. If, therefore, those who openly profess obedience are not {1131} required to obey absolutely in all things, then they do not differ in anything from those who do not vow obedience, and thus

---

[58] *Religiosi professi*. See note 37, supra.

[59] Colossians 3:20.

[60] *Regula*, ch. 68.

such a profession would be superfluous. Therefore, since it is not superfluous, then they are required to obey in all things.

But to the contrary, Bernard says,[61] "Nothing may hinder me from what I have promised, nothing more demanded than what I have promised." But nothing is promised except what is in the rules of the order. Therefore, the subject is not required to obey in matters other than those which relate to a rule.

Further, no one is held to anything to which others are not held, except insofar as he obligates himself specifically by a vow. But those who have professed do not vow obedience in all matters, but only to obey according to this or that rule. Therefore, they are not required to obey in all matters. And this reasoning is taken from the words of Bernard: "Enough that it is ordained to the will of the prelate that he who is professed solemnly pledges obedience; not, however, obedience in every case, but limited according to a rule, none other than that of Saint Benedict."[62] And again: "Let the prelate know for himself the standard set beforehand from the rule and thus keep his commands exclusively within the bounds of what alone has been established as correct, not anything correct, whatever you please, but only what [Benedict] established."

Solution

I respond by saying that obedience is three-fold, namely, undivided, imperfect and divided yet perfect. Undivided obedience, which ought not to be called obedience, occurs when anyone obeys in those things which are contrary to the divine rule of law which he ought to observe without violation, or even in those matters which are contrary to the rule he has professed to obey, at least in those which are not subject to a dispensation of the prelate. No one is held to this obedience. To the contrary, everyone is held not to have this sort of obedience. However, obedience which is imperfect, but sufficient for the salvation of those professing obedience, is that by virtue of which anyone obeys in these matters which he has promised to

---

[61] 2 _De disp. et praecepto_, ch. 5.

[62] _Ibid._, ch. 4.

observe, but not in others. Hence, Bernard says,[63] "For the rest, the subject will renew imperfect obedience of this kind, which is controlled by the aims of the vow." Those who profess obedience are restricted of necessity to this obedience. But perfect obedience is that according to which the subject obeys absolutely in all matters which are not contrary to divine law or to a rule which he has professed. Hence, Bernard says,[64] {1132} "Perfect obedience is ignorant of the law; it is not bent to certain limits, nor is it restrained within the narrow terms[65] of the profession. It is practised to the extent of charity . . . and for everything which is enjoined, it is extended to infinity by the spontaneous force of a free and lively spirit, giving no consideration to the mode." And no one is held to this obedience as due of necessity, but only out of a kind of nobility, just as one is always required to emulate the higher gifts. Nevertheless, certain persons say otherwise, namely, that those who vow obedience are of necessity required to obey their prelates not only in what pertains to the rule, but in all matters which are not contrary to the rule, whether they are matters which are neither good nor bad, or, as to certain types of good, so long as they are not higher than the vow of the particular order requires. But the prelate can compel those things which are equally great or easier to do, even if they are not according to the precepts of the rule. But the first opinion is better by far. This is so because, since the duty of obedience is caused by the order of an authority, the subject is obligated to that only by the vow of obedience, for which the authority is established. However, authorities are established in religious orders so that the condition of the order is preserved according to the precepts of the rule. And thus only in what pertains to a rule is the duty of obedience created. It is true, however, that something pertains to a rule in two senses: either directly or indirectly. Directly, such as in the sense of what is contained in the statutes of the rule, for example, not to eat meats, to keep silence, and the like. Indirectly, such as in the sense of what pertains to reciprocal

---

[63] Ibid., ch. 6.

[64] Ibid.

[65] Reading *angustiis* for *augustiis*.

services, without which the state of the religious order could not be maintained, or likewise, what pertains to the punishment of violations, though no specific mention of them be made in the rule.

I therefore respond to the first point by saying that the command of the Apostle is not to be understood absolutely as to all matters, but as to all which pertain to the superiority of the father over the child. This is so because, as the Philosopher says,[66] in certain matters the father is to be obeyed to a greater extent, in certain matters the leader of the army rather than the father, and in certain matters the doctor, and so also to others.

To the second point I respond that Benedict is speaking of perfect obedience which all who profess obedience are bound to emulate out of nobility. However, they are not obligated from necessity.

To the third point I respond that chastity is a virtue having a definite matter and a definite act, and similarly with poverty. In fact, obedience has a general matter, as was said. And thus, if anyone vows obedience absolutely {1133} in all matters, it would be a confusion of the religious orders, because one person would be required to observe the same as the other. And thus the vow of obedience is delimited in accordance with a firmly determined rule. However, it is not the same with the other two vows.

To the fourth point I respond that, although the subject is not to judge the command of the prelate, nevertheless, he is to judge concerning the particular act to the extent to which he is not subject to the prelate from the order of authority. And thus, it does not follow that he is to obey in all matters. To the contrary, it is necessary that he not obey in certain matters.

To the fifth point I respond that those who have not vowed obedience are not required to obey the spiritual prelates in all matters, except in those which pertain to the rule which they have professed in baptism, as for example, renouncing Satan and all his works, and vowing to lead a Christian life, they put on the new man, who is created in accordance with God.

---

[66]*Nicomachean Ethics*, Book 9, ch. 2.

Literal Exposition[67]

"Next something worthy of consideration presents itself." The reason for the order here is: because the potential is known through the act. Therefore, the determination of the act of sin has been prior to that of the potential for sin, although the potential is prior in itself[68] to the act.

"Whether the potential for sin arises in us from God or from ourselves." It seems that it ought to say potentials for sin, in the plural, because sinning occurs by the actions of several potentials. But it may be said that no potential possesses what elicits the act of sin except insofar as it is the will or is set in motion by the will, and thus there is one potential according to which sin consists principally, namely, will or free choice.[69]

"The morally bad will is not in us from God, but from ourselves and the devil." This is true, if the will is taken for the act of the will, but not if it is taken for the potential which is the principle of the act.[70] And thus there is no similarity through which they want to draw a conclusion concerning the potential from what is similar to it.

"However, it has been shown beyond doubt by the witness of many holy men that the power for evil does come from God." It seems that this proof of the Master is totally invalid. This is so because the authorities which follow are not speaking of the potential for sin, but of the power of sovereignty. However, it must be said that in the power for sovereignty, which is a characteristic potential,[71] there is also included a characteristic power for sin. This is so because, on account of the power of sovereignty, the sovereigns can commit many sins which they could not if they were not

---

[67]*Expositio textus*, i.e., exposition of the text.

[68]*Naturaliter prior.*

[69]*Voluntas vel liberum arbitrium.*

[70]*Principium actus.* Cf. note 23, supra.

[71]*Habitualis potentia.*

sovereigns.

"Through me kings reign, and through me rulers possess the earth." What the differences are between a king and a ruler is manifest from what is said in the Third Article of the First Question.[72]

"But it is known that the Apostle was speaking of secular authority." {1134} It seems that this solution of the Master is insufficient. This is so because earlier he showed that even the power for doing evil which the devil possesses is from God, and thus it seems that, if one is to obey a power because it comes from God, then the devil is to be obeyed. But it is said without a doubt that the authority[73] of the Apostle is to be understood only concerning the power of sovereignty. The devil does not have power of whatever kind over men, except insofar as they enter into a kind of compact with him, agreeing with him through sin to exist as his slaves. But this agreement is illicit. Thus an obligation of obedience is not acquired from it; rather, the pact is to be broken. "Your pact with the devil will not stand."[74] Hence, it is not proper that all power that comes from God be obeyed, but only that power which has been established by God for this, that the obedience due to itself is laid out. The power of sovereignty is alone this way.

"Reject the authority when greater powers are to be feared."[75] From this it appears that a greater power is to be obeyed to a greater extent than a lesser power.[76]

1. But this appears to be false. This is so because in certain things one is to be obeyed to a greater extent than another, and in certain things less

---

[72]See text at notes 33-34, supra.

[73]Auctoritas.

[74]Isaiah 27:18.

[75]Cf. Part I, note 18, supra.

[76]Mandonnet notes that an intended fourth article to the Second Question could be reconstructed here. See II Scriptum super Libros Sent., 44, expositio, n. 2.

so, as in certain matters more the father than the leader of the army, and in certain others the leader of the army more than the father, as is said in the Nicomachean Ethics.[77] Thus it follows that the same thing in the same place may be greater and lesser.

2. Further, the archbishop is a greater authority than the bishop. But in certain matters the subjects are required to obey the bishop to a greater extent than the archbishop. Thus a greater power is not always to be obeyed to a greater extent.

3. Further, abbots of monasteries are subject to the bishop, unless they are exempted. Therefore, the authority of the bishop is greater than that of the abbot. But the monk is required to obey the abbot to a greater extent than the bishop. Therefore, the greater authority is not always to be obeyed to a greater extent.

4. Further, the spiritual authority is higher than the secular. Thus, if the greater authority is to be obeyed to a greater extent, then the spiritual prelate will always be able to absolve us from a command of the secular authority, which is false.

I respond by saying that superior and inferior authority can exist in two ways. In the first case, it exists in such a way that the inferior authority proceeds from the superior entirely, and then the whole force of the inferior is based upon the force of the superior. Then the authority of the superior is to be obeyed absolutely and in all matters to a greater extent than {1135} the inferior, just as in natural things the first cause exercises a greater influence over what is caused by the second cause than the second cause itself.[78] And the authority of God is thus for every created authority, the authority of the emperor for the authority of the proconsul, the authority of the pope for every spiritual authority in the Church. This is so because from the pope himself the various degrees of official rank in the Church are both distributed and ordained. Hence, his authority is a certain foundation of the Church, as is clear in

---

[77]Book 9, ch. 2.

[78]The Latin text cites as authority the pseudo-Aristotelian work, Liber de Causis.

Matthew 16.[79] And thus, in all things we are required to obey the pope to a greater extent than the bishop or the archbishop or the monks the abbot, without any distinction. On the other hand, the superior and inferior authority can be such that both proceed from one certain supreme authority which subjects one to the other as it wills, and then the one is not superior to the other except in what the one is subordinated to the other by the supreme authority. In these matters only is the superior to be obeyed to a greater extent than the inferior, and in this way are the authorities of both the bishop and the archbishop proceeding from the authority of the pope.

I therefore respond to the first point by saying that it is not unfitting that the father is superior in family affairs and the leader in matters of war. But he who is superior in all things, namely God, is to be obeyed absolutely to a greater extent, and he who takes the place of God fully.

To the second point I respond that in those things in which the bishop is to be obeyed to a greater extent than the archbishop, the archbishop is not superior to the bishop, but solely in cases determined by the law, in which it is returned to the archbishop from the bishop.

To the third point I respond that the monk is required to obey the abbot to a greater extent than the bishop in those things which pertain to the statutes of the rule. However, in things which pertain to ecclesiastical discipline the bishop is to be obeyed to a greater extent, because in these things the abbot is subject to the bishop.

To the fourth point I respond that both the spiritual and the secular authorities are derived from divine authority. Thus, so far as the secular is below the spiritual, to that extent it is subordinated to it by God, namely, in matters which pertain to the salvation of the soul. And thus in these things the spiritual authority is to be obeyed to a greater extent than the secular. However, in matters which pertain to civil welfare, the secular authority is to be obeyed to a greater extent than the spiritual: "Render unto

---

[79]Matthew 16:18-19 is probably intended.

Caesar the things that are Caesar's."[80] Unless, perhaps,[81] the secular authority {1136} is conjoined to the spiritual authority, as in the pope, who holds the crown of each authority, spiritual and secular, the matter being arranged that way, he is priest and king,[82] priest forever, according to the order of Melchisedech, King of kings, Lord of lords, whose authority will not be withdrawn and whose kingdom not be destroyed, now and forever. Amen.

---

[80]Matthew 22:21.

[81]<u>Nisi forte</u>. The use of this expression may be of some significance, given its place in the argumentation. What follows the expression appears to undercut the cogency of what has just been established, i.e., the primacy of the pope may negate the previously expressed notion that the spiritual power is not necessarily superior to the secular. Deferrari points out that <u>nisi forte</u> is sometimes used ironically by Aquinas. Deferrari, <u>Latin-English Dictionary</u>, p. 700, s.v. "nisi."

[82]<u>Sacerdos et rex</u>.

PART III

EXCERPTS FROM THE COMMENTARY OF BONAVENTURE

PART III

EXCERPTS FROM THE COMMENTARY OF BONAVENTURE[1]

Commentary on the Second Book of the Sentences of Master Peter Lombard: Distinction 44

Textual Analysis[2]

Previously the Master indicated how sin has its beginning in the will, in general and in particular. In this part he determines wherein the potential for sin[3] has its beginning, and this part continues to the end of the book.[4]

This part is divided into four sections. In the first the Master examines whence comes the potential for sin, and he determines that, in the opinion of some, the potential for sin is not from God. In the second section he shows that all power[5] is from God, by many authorities,[6] at the place where he says, "However, it has been shown beyond doubt by the witness of many holy men," and so forth. In the third section he considers a particular doubt which has its origin in the preceding discussion, namely, whether any power[7] is

---

[1] This translation is based upon the following text: Bonaventure, <u>Opera Theologica Selecta</u>, vol. 2: <u>Sententiarum Liber II</u> (Florence: Typographia Collegii S. Bonaventurae, 1938), pp. 1040-59.

[2] <u>Divisio Textus</u>. Cf. Part II, note 2, supra.

[3] <u>Potentia peccandi</u>. Unlike Aquinas, Bonaventure makes no consistent use of extensively shaded Latin terms of art approximating the English "power." Cf. Part II, note 3, supra.

[4] I.e., to the end of the Second Book.

[5] <u>Omnis potentia</u>.

[6] <u>Auctoritatibus</u>.

[7] <u>Potestati</u>.

to be resisted, at the place where he says, "Here a question is asked." There he determines that at some times it should be obeyed, at others resisted. In the fourth and last section the Master continues the discourse, so that it passes from this book to the third one, at the place where he says, "Until now we directed the entire attention of the mind," and so forth. This last small section could be separated from the whole preceding part, but on account of its brevity it has not been split off. In this way, therefore, the details of the divisions are more a matter of curiosity than utility, and for that reason I have passed over them in the preceding discussion.

Treatment of the Questions[8]

For an understanding of this part, this inquiry breaks into three questions.

First, it is asked wherein the power for sin[9] has its origin.

Second, it is asked whence a power arises in man for governing or ruling.[10]

Third, a question is asked about the necessity for being subject to the power for governing.

Concerning the first question, two points are raised. First, it is asked whether the potential for sin[11] arises in man from God or from man himself. Second, it is asked whether the potential for sin, such as it is, is good or evil.

---

[8]<u>Tractatio Quaestionum</u>.

[9]<u>Potestas peccandi</u>.

[10]<u>Potestas praesidendi sive dominandi</u>.

[11]<u>Potentia peccandi</u>.

Article I

In what does the power for sin have its origin

Question I

Whether the potential for sin arises in us from God. Thus we proceed to the first question. And it appears that:

1. By the authority of Augustine concerning the psalms, the Master leads to the following passage: "The will for wickedness can arise from the soul of man, but the power only from God." But the will for wickedness, which arises in man from himself, does not arise except with regard to evil whereby one sins. Therefore, if with regard to that same thing the power arises from God, it seems that the power for sin arises from God in himself. {1041}[12]

2. Likewise, the Philosopher says,[13] "God and the zealot can do depraved things." But everything in which man shares with God he has of itself from a cause and a principle. Just so therefore, if in the potential for sin man shares with God, it seems that he receives the potential for sin from God.

3. Likewise, everything which confirms the excellence of nature is from God. But the power for sin in the one in whom it exists confirms the excellence of nature. For it cannot be found except in the rational creature, which is the most excellent of all creatures.

4. Likewise, everything which contributes to the amplification of praise is from God, of whom all honor and praise is. But to be capable of sin contributes to the praise of the just man, as is said in Ecclesiastes, "He who could have transgressed and has not trans-

---

[12]Bracketted numbers in the text refer to page numbers of the *Opera Theologica Selecta* edition, note 1, supra.

[13]The Latin edition gives the reference *Topics*, Book 4, ch. 5, but this appears incorrect. Further, the text has *stodiosus*, but should read *studiosus*, the Latin equivalent of the Aristotelian *spoudaios*.

gressed, and could have done evil and did not."[14] Therefore, it seems that the capability for sin in man comes from God.

5. Likewise, the potential for sin is in the rational creature either in accordance with what is from God or in accordance with what is from nothing. If the former, I have attained the proposition, namely, that man receives such a potentiality from God. If the latter, then, since every creature comes from nothing, each has the potentiality for sin. If then, this is false, the proposition remains, and so forth.

But to the contrary, a. To sin is to fail. But to fail or fall short is an incapability and a privation of potentiality. If, then, privation and failing of potentiality are not from God, it seems that the potential for sin does not arise in man from God, but rather from himself.

b. Likewise, act and potential are from the same principle.[15] Therefore, if sin is not from God in any way, then neither is the potential for sin in man from God.

c. Likewise, grace is perfecting and saving of nature. But through grace the potential for sin is removed. If, then, grace does not remove what God gave, it seems that man does not receive the potential for sin from God.

d. Likewise, the potential for sin is the potential for acting against God. Therefore, the potential for sin, insofar as it is of this kind, opposes the divine potential. If, then, the divine potential does nothing against itself, it seems that the potential for sin does not arise from it.

e. Likewise, everything which is in man from God has an exemplar in God. But the potential for sin, insofar as it is of this kind, does not have an exemplar in God. For it is impossible that God might sin,[16] and it is impossible for an exemplar in God to

---

[14]Ecclesiastes 31:10.

[15]_Ab eodem principio_.

[16]The text cites Augustine's _De Symbolo_, sermo ad

have a defect. If, then, man is not assimilated to God in the potential for sin, but on the contrary is assimilated to the devil, and everything man has from God he has in exemplarity and similarity itself, it seems that the potential for sin in man does not have its cause and origin from God.

Response. I respond by saying that, when I speak of the potential for sin, I speak of two things. I speak both of some potential and of a potential directed to such an act. If, then, we speak about the potential for sin, as to what is potential, then that potential is the free choice of the will, thus without a doubt it is from God. However, if we speak of the capacity of that potential for being directed[17] toward sin, then what is spoken of is: that sin is received in a sense abstractly, in a sense concretely. In a sense it names the deformed act, in a sense the deformity itself. Thus, we speak in a two-fold sense of the capacity for being directed {1042} toward sin: either with respect to the deformity or with respect to the underlying act.[18] If the latter, such a capacity is thus from God, as for example the underlying act of sin. If, however, we speak of that capacity with respect to the deformity, then, since that deformity is nothing other than a privation and a defect, such a capacity is nothing other than a deficiency. And so, just as the defect of the deformity is not from God, neither is such a deficiency from God, but is in the rational creature itself, because it is from nothing. Thus, then, the potential for sin in one way is admitted to be from God, in another way not at all. And in accordance with this, the reasons run for the opposing side, and still there have been differing opinions.

For, as the Master says in his writings, some have said that the potential for sin is not from God, while others have said that it is from God, which the Master endeavors to prove by many authorities. However, these authorities are not strong enough for reaching this conclusion, unless the potential for sin were taken as

---

Catechum., c. 1, n.2; 83 Quaest., qq. 3 and 21; De civitate Dei, 5:10.

[17]De ordinabilitate.

[18]Respectu actionis substratae.

that which is, or with respect to the act for which it is, because in this way it is included under the genus of potentiality. However, as the potential for sin is considered in comparison with the deformity itself, it is thus not in the genus of potentiality, but to the conrtary, of impotency. Thus, it is not called potential but defect. And, just as it does not follow that, since God can do all things, he can sin, thus it does not follow by that method that, since every power[19] comes from God, the power for sin is from God. And in that way Anselm says that "The power for sin is not freedom nor a part of freedom."[20] And in this way, the reasoning proceeds, showing that the power for sin is not in man from God, and thus the arguments are to be conceded.

1. As to what is objected concerning the potential for evil,[21] to the effect that it is from God, although the will does not arise from him, I respond as follows. In that passage Augustine was forcefully making the distinction between the potential itself, by which one sins, and the direction, in the sense of an action,[22] by which one sins. He wishes to say that the potential itself comes from God, although the disposition toward sin is not, since it is an indisposition[23] rather than a disposition. And so from this the proposition is not reached, except that the potential for sin, with respect to what is, comes from God. With respect to what is for sin, however, it cannot be elicited from that authority that it comes from God, rather the opposite, since the potential for sin does not amount to sin except through the medium of voluntary disorder or indisposition, which Augustine in the above citation denies is from God.

2. As to that passage from the Philosopher in which he says that God and the zealot can do what is

---

[19] Omnis potestas.

[20] De. Lib. arb., ch. 1.

[21] De potentia nocendi.

[22] Actualem ordinationem. Cf. Roy J. Deferrari, A Latin-English Dictionary of St. Thomas Aquinas (Boston: St. Paul Editions, 1960), s.v. "ordinatio."

[23] Deordinatio.

perverse, some explain that the Philosopher was thinking of the evil that consists of punishment.[24] But this is plainly inconsistent with his text. And so, since the sacred scripture says, and all the commentators are in accord, that in no way can [God] sin, just as he can neither deceive nor deny himself,[25] I respond by saying that that passage from the Philosopher is bereft of truth. Nor do I believe this view to be very emphatically presented in that passage, since he said it solely by way of example in passing. And his example sufficed for the proposition for that part which is true, namely, as to the fact that the zealot can do evil things, granting that this is not insofar as he is a zealot, but insofar as he can fall short of virtue.

3. As to what is objected to the effect that the potential for sin confirms the excellence of nature, I respond by saying that this is not true, insofar as it speaks of the disposition with reference to the defect, but rather, insofar as {1043} it speaks of the disposition toward the underlying act. For no act is deformable through fault except that which proceeds from a deliberative potential, which is excellent, because that alone is informable by justice. Alternatively, I respond that to confirm the excellence of something is two-fold: either essentially or accidentally.[26] The potential for sin and sin confirm the excellence of nature accidentally, as Augustine says,[27] "Sorrow over the good that is lost is a witness of good nature."

4. As to what is objected, to the effect that it acts for the amplification of praise, I respond by saying that, just as a more commendable virtue is gained from sins, so a more commendable potential for doing good is gained from the potential to do evil. This is so not because some vice augments the good of virtue, nor some potential for failing [augments] the potential for doing good, but rather because from the presence of an opposite it becomes clearer in its goodness. Thus, the virtuousness of a man is more

---

[24] De malo poenae, as opposed to malum culpae. Cf. Deferrari, A Latin-English Dictionary, s.v. "malum."

[25] 2 Timothy 2:13.

[26] Aut per se aut per accidens.

[27] De civitate Dei, 19:13.

apparent when he can, but does not wish to, do evil, than if he neither could nor wishes to do so. And so the just man is praised in that he could do evil and did not. He is praised in that he did good and not evil though he could. Thus, that praise relates more essentially to the fact that he is doing good. It does not relate to the fact that he is capable of sinning, except accidentally. Hence, the potential for doing evil having been circumscribed, if he did good voluntarily, he would yet be praised.

5. As to what is asked concerning whether the potential for sin exists in the creature from God or from nothing, I respond by saying that, with respect to the concept of the underlying act, which is the deliberative act, it exists in him from God, but with respect to the defect it exists in him from nothing. And hence it is that the potential for sin is not found in every creature, because it is not found in the irrational creature on account of its imperfections, for which reason there cannot exist in it an act of deliberation. It is not found in the blessed creature on account of its perfection in every way, since there cannot exist in it a defect, to such an extent is it united to its creator. And thus the potential for sin in a certain sense is cancelled through grace; in a certain sense it is relinquished. In a certain sense it is freedom itself; in a certain sense it diminishes freedom. In a certain sense it is a potential and in a certain sense an impotency, because in a certain sense it speaks of affirmation, and in another of a privation. And so, when it is asked whether it comes from God, it is not to be answered, except in accordance with the distinction discussed above.

Question II

Whether the potential for sin, understood in that way, is evil. Second, it is asked whether the potential for sin, understood in that way, is evil. And it appears that it is evil.

1. The potential for sin is nothing other than the will. But the will for sin is evil. Therefore, the potential for sin is evil, understood in that sense.

2. Likewise, anything the use of which is evil, is also itself evil. But the use of the potential for sin is sin, and to sin is evil. And therefore the

potential for sin is evil.

3. Likewise, just as the potential for doing good consists in itself of the good, so also the potential for doing evil of the evil. But every potential for doing good, understood in that sense, is good. Therefore the potential for doing evil is in that sense evil.

4. Likewise, each potential is more complete the more it is united to its act. But the potential for doing evil, when united to the act of doing evil, is evil. Therefore, if {1044} the less complete it is, the more separated from the act, it thus appears that it is separated from the act of evil.

5. Likewise, the potential for doing evil is either good or bad. If it is good, and every good is in and from God, then it seems that the potential for doing evil, understood in that way, both comes from and exists in God, both of which are false. Hence, it remains that the potential for sin is evil.

But to the contrary, a. If the potential for sin is evil, then the ability to sin is evil. But a just and holy man can sin; therefore, the just and holy man is evil.

b. Likewise, if the potential for sin is evil, then it is by way of either an evil of punishment or an evil of deliberate fault or guilt. It is not the former, because that follows from the latter. It is not the latter, because fault or guilt is the consequent of the potential for sin in time and by nature. Yet both man and the angel could sin prior to either sinning.

c. Likewise, if the potential for sin is evil, then either there is a malice which it effects or it is a malice which is effected by itself. The former is not reasonable, because many can do evil who do not and have not done so. The latter is countered by Augustine, who proves that man can do evil by no other author than himself.[28] Therefore, it does not seem that the potential for sin, as it is of itself,[29] is

---

[28] 83 Quaestionum.

[29] Quantum est de se.

evil.

    d. Likewise, it does not follow that, if one can commit adultery, then one is an adulterer. Thus it does not follow that, if one can do evil, then one is evil. But, if the potential for doing evil were evil, then it necessarily would follow that it would be evil itself, and so forth.

    Along with this, it is asked, whence it is that the will to do evil is evil, and the potential for doing evil is said not to be evil? Furthermore, it is asked, on what account is the will for sin not said to be a lack of the will, just as the potential for sin is said to be an impotency? For that seems to be the case even more so. For if the will for sin is said to be a greater approximation to the defect of sin than the potential for sin is, then it appears even more so that the will for sin be said to be a lack of will than that the potential for sin be called an impotency.

    <u>Response</u>. I respond by saying that, just as a potential with respect to good things is not said to be the direction in the sense of an action[30] for an effect, but only in the sense of a state,[31] while the will is said to be the direction in the sense of an action, so also with respect to evil things it is to be understood that the potential is not said to be the direction in the sense of an action for the defect, but rather in the sense of a state. Hence, one is not said to possess a potential for doing evil because one actually directs oneself into evil. However, the will is said to be the direction in the sense of an action. For it is not said that one wills evil except to the extent that one actually directs oneself to evil. For, just as was said in the first book,[32] the will is the approximation of its own potential to action. And thus, because to be evil is said to be a certain defect present in or around that of which it is said, hence it is that the will for sin is evil, and to will to sin is evil, while the potential for sin, or the capability to

---

[30] See note 22, supra.

[31] <u>Habitualem</u> [<u>ordinationem</u>]. Cf. Deferrari, <u>A Latin-English Dictionary</u>, s.v. "ordinatio."

[32] I.e., in the first book of Bonaventure's commentary, Distinction 45,2,1.

sin is not said to be evil. Consequently, the arguments demonstrating that the potential for sin, understood in that way, is not evil are to be conceded.

1. As to what is first objected to the contrary concerning the will, I respond by saying that that is of no use, because the will for doing evil determines more than the potential for doing evil. For it is said to be the direction in the sense of an action for evil, or as I may say particularly, an actual disordering. Hence, just as that argument is of no use which states, "to will to do evil is evil, therefore to be able to do evil is evil," so neither is it of any use to argue {1045} that the potential to do evil is nothing other than the will. Although it is no other, nevertheless, in one way the term "potential" is introduced through this, and in another way the term "will," because in the one it is introduced in the withdrawal of a greater, and in the other in the approximation of the greater. And thus, there is a sophism of the accident,[33] just as here: it is the same will which is separated from evil and which is brought close to evil; therefore, if evil is just as it is when approached, from a comparison with evil, similarly evil will be just as it is at a distance. For here something is ascribed similarly to belong to the accident and to the subject thing.

2. As to what is objected, to the effect that the exercise of the potential for sin, understood as such, is evil, I respond by saying that that is understood especially as to the exercise to which each and everything is directly and proximately ordered. But the potential for sin is ordained neither directly nor proximately to the act of sin, for which that same potential is ordained to and for its opposite _per se_. However, for this it is ordained accidentally. Hence, the opposite of sin is its use and sin is its abuse. And thus it does not follow that, if to sin is evil, the potential for sin, understood as such, is evil because of this.

3. As to what is objected, to the effect that in good things the potential for doing good is good, and

---

[33]_Sophisma secundum accidens_, i.e., the fallacy in which an accident is taken as if it belonged to the subject of necessity. Cf. Deferrari, _A Latin-English Dictionary_, s.v. "sophisma."

so forth, I respond by saying that it is not the same, because in good things the goodness of the act is from the goodness of the potential. Hence, it is often said that, not because we do good we are good, but because we are good, we do good. However, it is not the same with evil things, but the contrary, because we do we evil, we are evil. And the reason for this is, because, although the potential cannot perfect itself through its act, still it can disorder itself and make itself deficient through its act. And so a good deed does not so much add to the deed as to the character of merit, just as sin adds not so much to the sin as to the character of demerit.

4. As to what is objected, to the effect that a potential is more complete when it is joined to its act, I respond by saying that this is true as to the act to which it is ordained absolutely. But it is not true of that to which it is ordained accidentally, especially when that act is understood more under the concept of a defect than of an effect. For then it is more disordered than perfected, and thus it is for the potential for sin with regard to the act of sin. Thus, the potential falls short of completion in that one sins, rather than in that one could sin.

5. As to what is asked concerning whether the potential for sin is good or bad, I respond by saying that, if the potential for sin is said to be a potential by which anyone can sin, without a doubt it is good and is from God. Similarly, if the potential for sin is said to be directed to the underlying act for sin, it is from God. If, however, the potential for sin is said to be the power for failing, in this way it ought not to be said to be good or evil. It ought not to be said to be good, because it is not said of some being, and nothing possesses the concept of being that does not possess the concept of the good. It ought not to be said to be evil, because it is not said to consist by nature in the privation of some good, nor is it said to be an actual defect but a disposition. Hence, such a potential ought not to be said to be an evil or deficient potential, but an impotency. Hence, just as it is neither good nor evil to be incapable of seeing through a stone, because it cannot be said to be by nature either an affirmation or a privation, so also it is to understood as to the potential for sin in the rational creature, according to which it has being out of nothing.

From this the response is evident to what was last asked, namely, why the will for sin is said (1046) to be evil and not the power. For it is the will that is the immediate cause and closest to the act, which proceeds from deliberation. However, the potential for sin is more properly said to be an impotency than the will for sin can be said to be an involuntariness, in view of the fact that the term "potential" is bestowed from affirmation and completion. And so, sinning diminishes the concept of the potential, since it speaks of a defect, just as death diminishes the concept of man. However, the term "will" is bestowed from freedom and satisfaction. And because sin is agreeable and has to be committed through a free choice, from this cause it is a fact that, although it may corrupt the potential of the will, nevertheless it does not diminish the concept of the will, because it does not have a repugnance for itself in accordance with what is thus named. And on that account, to will to sin is to will, although to be able to sin is not to be capable. And thus it was said in the first book of the Sentences[34] that God is all-powerful and yet he is not said to be all-willing.

Article II

Concerning the power for governing[35]

Consequently, questions are raised concerning the power for governing. And of this two things are asked. First, it is asked whether every potential for ruling[36] comes from God.

Second, it is asked whether the power for ruling[37] comes from God as a natural institution or as a punishment for guilt.

---

[34]Liber I Sent., 45,1,2.

[35]De potestate praesidendi.

[36]Omnis potentia dominandi.

[37]Potestas dominandi.

Question I

Whether every power for ruling[38] comes from God.

Of this first question we proceed to ask, whether the power for ruling comes from God. And as to that, it appears as follows.

1.[39] The Lord said to Pilate: "You would have no power over me, unless it were given to you from above."[40] Therefore, if the power of Pilate over Christ was from God, and yet it appeared least likely that he ought to have power over [Christ], then it seems much more forcefully to be the case that every such power is from God.

2. Likewise, it was more expressly said to the Romans, "There is no power except from God,"[41] and it is established that there he speaks of the power of governing.[42] Therefore, and so forth. And those two authorities are sufficient, since many others are cited in the literature.

3. Likewise, this itself appears by reason. The power for governing is said to be potential in excellence, and every such thing is said to be an affirmation of some kind. But everything which is said to be an affirmation of some kind comes from the highest power.[43] Therefore, every potential for governing comes from God, who rules in whatever way is involved.

4. Likewise, every punishment comes from God which has the form of punishment absolutely. But every servitude is a punishment. Therefore, it is from God. But by the same reasoning, the power for ruling is also a punishment. Hence, every power for ruling is from

---

[38]*Potestas dominandi*. Cf. note 36, supra.

[39]The Latin text uses letters for this series, a use which is inconsistent with the convention used throughout the rest of the commentary.

[40]John 19:11.

[41]Romans 13:1.

[42]*De potestate praesidendi*.

[43]*A summa potentia*.

God.

But to the contrary, a.[44] It is written that "They have set up kings, but not by me; they have appointed princes, but I did not know it."[45] Therefore, it appears that such presidence of the wicked does not come from God.

b. Likewise, nothing unjust comes from God. But many are unjustly ruled by others. Therefore, it appears that not every authority or civil power[46] that is over men comes from God.

c. Likewise, nothing disordered comes from God. But, when the foolish are placed in authority over the wise, and the evil over the good, this is disordered. Therefore, it does not appear to be from God.

d. Likewise, nothing that is contrary to natural law is from God. But the power for ruling over men is contrary to natural law. Therefore, it is not from God. The major premiss is manifest. The minor is proven by what is written in the {1047} Institutes, "Wars have arisen, and captivity and slavery have followed, which are contrary to natural law."[47]

e. Likewise, nothing that is to be refrained from is anything that is given by God. Therefore, if every power or authority[48] is from God, nothing that is to be removed is an authority or power. Therefore, no sovereign[49] or prince may be deposed, however much evil he may be.

---

[44]The Latin text uses numbers, instead of letters, for this series, a use which is inconsistent with the convention used throughout the rest of the commentary. Cf. note 39, supra.

[45]Hosea 8:4.

[46]<u>Omnis potestas sive dominium</u>. Cf. Part II, note 3, supra.

[47]<u>Ius autem gentium</u>, Book I, tit. 2, sec. 2. (The Institutes form a part of the <u>Corpus Juris Civilis</u>.)

[48]<u>Omnis potestas vel praelatio</u>.

[49]<u>Praelatus</u>.

f. Likewise, nothing that anyone possessed by the donation of God is possessed by usurpation. Therefore, if every power is bestowed by God, no power is usurped. But it is plain that many powers are usurped. Therefore, not every power is given by God.

Response. I respond by saying that the power of governing is said to be that by which someone governs and has dominion over others. However, that by which one governs can be spoken of in two ways. In one way, it is said to be the capacity itself through which someone prevails over others, and this capacity is, without a doubt, from God. In another way, that by which one governs is said to be the mode of arriving at or continuing this excellence of capacity. And thus it is to be distinguished. For some preside over others out of justice, some from cunning, and some from violence. However, when someone presides over others through justice, then that power for ruling, absolutely speaking, is from God, both as to him who presides and as to those who are subject to him. When, however, someone presides through cunning or violence, then it is said that such power has to be placed in reference both to the will of him who presides and to the merit of the subject. In relation to the merit of the subject, such presidence is just when it is either for the testing of the good subjects or for the punishment of the evil. However, if it is compared to the will of him who presides, then it is unjust. And indeed the first way is said to be done and ordained by God, as is said: "He makes the hypocrite to reign on account of the sins of the people,"[50] and again, "I gave them a king in my anger."[51] However, in the second way, in relation to the will of him who presides, it is said to be with the permission of God, but not with his approval, as has been said: "They have set up kings, but not by me; they have appointed princes, but I did not know it."[52]

Accordingly, it is to be conceded that every power for governing, according to what it is and also with regard to him over whom it is exercised, is just and from God. And the reasons and authorities which are

---

[50] Job 34:30.

[51] Hosea 13:11.

[52] Hosea 8:4.

introduced in the first part show this, and thus these are to be conceded. Nevertheless, it is to be conceded that the mode of arriving at presidence, in relation to the will of him who presides, can be just or unjust. To the extent that it is just, it is from God; to the extent it is unjust, it is not from God. Because in fact from one side it is thus never unjust, but that it is just on the other, it can be said of no potential for governing that it does not proceed from God.

1. As to what is first objected to the contrary, that the Lord said that they have set up kings, but not by him, I respond by saying that there it is not the negation of any will, but of the preceding will and the approving will. For the civil power of evil persons is from an avenging God, rather than being from an accepting God. Hence, that which is said, "Wherein man has exercised authority over man to his harm,"[53] is verified in these evil persons.

2. As to what is objected, to the effect that nothing unjust is from God, I respond by saying that that is true, so far as what is unjust. Although the potential for ruling may frequently be unjust in relation to the will of him who presides, still it is always just in {1048} relation to the merit of the subject, because it is for the punishment of evildoers and for the praise of the good, as is said by Peter.[54]

3. As to what is objected, to the effect that some power is unordained, I respond by saying that,

---

[53] Ecclesiastes 8:9. The full text reads: "All this I have seen and applied my mind to every deed that has been done under the sun wherein man has exercised authority over another man to his hurt." Earlier in the same chapter, it is stated: "Since the word of the king is authoritative, who will say to him, 'What are you doing?' He who keeps a royal command experiences no trouble, for a wise heart knows the proper time and procedure." <u>Ibid</u>. 8:4-5.

[54] 1 Peter 2:14. The original text of Peter is ambiguous with respect to the proposition stated in the text of Bonaventure. It states: "Submit yourselves for the Lord's sake to every human institution, whether to a king as the one in authority, or to governors as sent by him for the punishment of evildoers and the praise of those who do right." 1 Peter 2:13-14.

even if in some fashion some power could proceed from a disordered will, still the power itself is always ordained, as Gregory says, "The exaltation of pride, not the ordinance of power, is to be blamed. God granted the potential; the wickedness of our mind discovered the exaltation of that potential."[55] And if it is objected that it is disordered that the foolish rule over the wise, the evil over the good, and the slave over the free, I respond by saying that, even if some disorder is externally apparent, nevertheless a pleasing order is hidden within in accordance with a divine judgment that is often hidden but never unjust. Because of what is said in Ecclesiastes, "I have seen an evil like an error that goes forth from the ruler, folly set in an exalted place,"[56] and so forth, as if to say: because, although there appears to be error there, still there is great order there, so long as the evil are punished and the good are improved.

4. As to what is objected, to the effect that there is no power from God which is contrary to natural law, I respond by saying that to be contrary to natural law is two-fold, either absolutely or according to some condition. Therefore, if it is said that the power for ruling is contrary to natural law, this is not to be understood as concerning the universal dictate of nature, but the natural dictate of some determined condition, in which there may indeed be no subjection to servitude nor authority of power.

5. As to what is objected, to the effect that nothing that is given by God is to be removed, I respond by saying that that is true, if God gave it absolutely. If, however, it is given solely for a time, just as the Lord wished to give it, so he still wished to remove it through human service. However, we know that God wishes this, since we see the order of justice thus determined. For God gave life to the brigand, and still the judge may justly take that from

---

[55]In Moralibus 26:26. For a continuation of this quotation, see Part I, text at note 14, supra.

[56]Ecclesiastes 10:5-6. This quotation appears to be a paraphrase. The full quotation is as follows: "There is an evil I have seen under the sun, like an error which goes forth from the ruler -- folly is set in many exalted places while rich men sit in humble places."

him, demanding the mandate of justice, as is said, "The evildoer shall not be allowed to live."[57] Still, it is to be understood that it is thus with our power and that of the leaders, because in accordance with the measures of the law, he who abuses the power granted to him deserves just as much to lose dominion as the privileges of power.

6. As to what is objected, to the effect that no power granted by God is usurped, I respond by saying that that is true, if it were given by God totally. But God gives power in such a way that frequently a man may be overwhelmed in the attainment of that power. When he is rightly overwhelmed for the attainment of power, then he is said to be ruled from justice. When in fact unjustly, the power is usurped, in that he does not preside de jure but de facto. Nevertheless, because such power is not altogether without the order of justice, it is conceded to be from God. And at the same time these two propositions are true, in different respects, namely, that the same power may be usurped and granted by God, without any incompatibility.

Question II

Whether the power for governing[58] is in man as a natural institution or as a punishment for guilt. Second, it is asked whether the power for governing is in man as a natural institution or as a punishment for guilt. And as to the first mode, it appears as follows. {1049}

1. "Let us make man in our image and likeness, and let him rule,"[59] and so forth. If you say that he had authority with respect to the beasts, but not with respect to men,[60] the point will not be escaped there-

---

[57]Exodus 22:18.

[58]Potestas praesidendi. Cf. note 37, supra.

[59]Genesis 1:26. This partial quotation is misleading when compared with the full text of the quoted verse, as follows: "Let Us make man in Our image, according to Our likeness; and let them rule over the fish of the sea and over the birds of the air and over every creeping thing that creeps on the earth."

[60]Cf. note 59, supra.

by, because it is said, "Man is the head of the woman."[61] If, therefore, the head rules the body and ought to rule the body, then it appears that the power for ruling arises in humankind as a natural institution.

2. Likewise, among the angels, who are perfect in nature and in grace, not only is there an order and degree as to excellence of natures, but even as to presidence of functions.[62] Therefore, it appears that civil authority is not incompatible, but is consonant with, a natural institution, human as well as angelic.

3. Likewise, the power for ruling is a property of dignity and nobility. But, if anything is fitting to a lapse of nature, so much more is it to a natural institution. It therefore appears that the power for ruling extends to the state of a natural institution more than to the state of a fallen nature.

4. Likewise, everything that is for the conservation of the natural order extends to a natural institution. But the power for governing pertains to the conservation of the natural order. Therefore, the power for governing is in man from God as a natural institution. The major premiss is manifest. The minor is proven by what Augustine says: "Penal servitude is ordained by the law which commands that the natural order be preserved and forbids it to be disturbed."[63] But the power for ruling and penal servitude are ordained for the same thing, and therefore the rest follows.

But to the contrary, a. Gregory says, "All men by nature are made equal, but the secret yet just dispensation of God prefers some to others according to various merits."[64] Therefore, it appears that submission and authority are not in man as a natural institution.

---

[61] 1 Corinthians 11:3.

[62] See Part II, note 32, supra.

[63] De civitate Dei 19:15.

[64] In Moralibus 21:15.

b. Likewise, Augustine says,[65] "God did not wish rational man, made in the image of God, to be ruled, only the irrational." Therefore, if the power for governing and ruling is in one man with respect to others, then it appears, and so forth.

c. Likewise, it appears thus by reason. Freedom is in man by nature, but the power for ruling is obstructive of freedom. Therefore, it does not appear that it arises by nature. Moreover, the fact that freedom both arises by nature and is impeded by the power for govering is manifest, because freedom is to be defined as follows:[66] "Freedom is a natural power by which man is permitted to do what he wishes."

d. Likewise, man, as to his first condition, is made in God's image, but insofar as he is the image of God, he was born to be carried in a direct way to God. Therefore, if God alone is greater than him, then in accordance with nature nothing is above man but God. Therefore, no civil power is in man as a natural institution except divine authority alone.

e. Likewise, there is no master without a slave; therefore, neither is there civil authority without servitude.[67] But servitude is introduced through sin, as Augustine says in many places.[68] Therefore, it appears that the power for ruling is in man as a condition of guilt, not as a natural institution.

f. Likewise, in the glorification of men "faults will be removed and nature will be retained."[69]   {1050}

---

[65] De civitate Dei 19:15.

[66] Justinian, Instit. iur. civ. 1:3, sec. 2.

[67] Bonaventure's statement of this argument here seems to be in part linguistic. He appears to draw a parallel between dominus (the master) and dominium (civil power), which respectively require servus (a slave) and servitus (servitude).

[68] The original text cites De civitate Dei 19:15; De Gen. ad lit. 11:37; and, Quaest. in Pentateuch I, q. 153. See Bonaventure, Opera Theologica Selecta, 2:1049, n. 3.

[69] De civitate Dei 22:17.

But in the state of grace the civil power of authority and the subjection of servitude will not remain. Therefore, these do not appear to be in human nature with respect to what is ordained, but only with respect to what is failed or corrupted.

Response. I respond by saying that the power for ruling or governing is said to be three-fold, namely, in the broadest sense, in common, and in its proper sense. In the broadest sense, the power for ruling is used with respect to everything which man can use at will and for his own desire. In this way, it is said that man is master of his possessions, whether movable or immovable. In another way, the power for ruling or governing is said to be the excellence of power in commanding that which is fit for reason or direction. In the third way, the power for ruling is said to be a power for coercing subjects. This power is said to be a certain stricture of freedom. Such a power for ruling is properly said to be dominion or civil power, to which the slave responds.

In the first way, the power for ruling is common to every state, namely the state of created nature, of fallen nature and nature glorified. In the second way, it corresponds to the state of the pilgrimage on earth,[70] either for the state of created nature or for the state of fallen nature. For if man had stood firm, the husband still could have commanded the wife and the father the son. And this is discerned also among the angels, inasmuch as it is said, "They are ministering angels,"[71] because on that part in another way they are in the state of the pilgrimage. Nevertheless, this presidence will not remain in the state of grace. . . . In fact, in this third way the power for ruling is in man only with regard to the state of fallen nature, for it exists for him as a punishment for sin, not as a natural institution. This is so because the servitude corresponding to it, according to what the saints say, is the pain of sin. And because we speak here of the

---

[70]<u>Statui viae</u>. Cf. Deferrari, <u>A Latin-English Dictionary</u>, s.v. "status."

[71]Hebrews 1:14. The full text of this passage is more illustrative of the point made in the text: "Are they not all ministering spirits, sent out to render service for the sake of those who will inherent salvation?"

power for ruling in that way, on that account the reasons shown are to be conceded, that such a power does not exist in man according to his primary condition or according to the state of created nature.

1. Therefore, as to what is first objected to the contrary, from the text of Genesis and 1 Corinthians, now the response is clear. They proceed from the power for governing taken in the first and second sense, not the third. For, although a wife may be in a certain sense inferior to her husband by reason of being of a weaker sex, nevertheless, because she is created to be of assistance to him not as an attendant but as a companion, hence it is that, although he is said to be her head, he is still not called lord, because the one is not the handmaid to the other. And thus, the Master said before, in the Eighteenth Distinction, that woman was created for equality. Thus, she was formed from the man's side, and not from his feet or head, so that she appears to be the companion to the man, not the mistress or handmaid.

2. As to what is objected, to the effect that authority exists among the angels, now the response is clear. Although one presides over another, commands another and has authority over another to command certain things of him that pertain to the duty of ministry, nevertheless one angel is not said to be the servant of another. Thus, from this it cannot be concluded that the power for ruling to which servitude corresponds is in man as a condition of nature.

3. As to what is objected, to the effect that civil power is the property of excellence, I respond by saying that, although it may be a property of excellence in him who presides, still it is said to be an indignity to him who is subject. And thus by nature it can be appropriate for man with respect to {1051} the other inferior creatures, yet with respect to other men it is not appropriate by nature, but in a sense praeternaturally, namely, in punishment of sin. For as Ambrose says,[72] servitude was introduced through the sin of drunkeness.

4. As to what is objected, to the effect that civil power and servitude were made for the conservation of the natural order, I respond by saying that

---

[72] De Elia et ieiunio 5:11.

there is an order which considers nature according to every state, and an order which considers nature according to the state of its corruption. And according to this, there are some of the prescription of nature absolutely, some in accordance with the state of created nature, some in accordance with the state of fallen nature. Nature in accordance with every state dictates that God is to be honored. In accordance with the state of created nature, it dictates that all things are in common. In accordance with the state of fallen nature, it dictates that something is one's own, to remove quarrels and struggles. Thus nature in accordance with every state dictates that all men are servants of God. In accordance with the state of his first condition, it dictates that man in fact is to be made equal to man. However, in accordance with the state of corruption, it dictates that man is to be subject to man and is to be a servant of man, so that the evil are repressed and the good are defended. For unless there are civil powers of this kind coercing the evil, because of the corruption which exists in nature, one might oppress another, and men could not live together. Nevertheless, it would not have been thus if man had remained in the state of innocence, for everyone would have maintained his position and state. And thus it is clear that that reasoning does not lead to the conclusion that servitude or dominion refers to created nature, but only to fallen nature, where order has been disturbed and can be conserved through dominion.

Article III

Concerning the necessity for subjection to the governing power[73]

Consequently, questions are raised concerning the necessity for being subject to the governing power. And on this two things are asked.

First, it is asked whether Christians are required to be subject to rulers[74] in some things.

---

[73] Potentiae praesidendi.

[74] Tyrannis. Cf. Part I, note 10, supra.

Second, it is asked whether the religious[75] are required to be subject to their prelates in all things.

Question I

Whether Christians are required to be subject to rulers or a secular power in some things. As to this first question, we proceed as follows and ask whether Christians are required to be subject to rulers or a secular power in some things. And it appears that:

1.[76] "Servants be submissive to your masters with all respect, not only to those who are good and gentle, but also to those who are unreasonable."[77]

2. Likewise, "Let every person be in subjection to the governing authorities."[78] And thereafter: "Render to all what is due them, tax to whom tax is due, custom to whom custom."[79] And if you say that this is an admonition for avoiding scandal, to the contrary Paul says before that: "It is necessary to be in subjection, not only because of wrath but also for conscience' sake."[80]

3. Likewise, this is shown by the reason which the Apostle gives in the same passage.[81] "There is," he says, "no authority except from God, and those which exist are established by God." Therefore, every power

---

[75]*Religiosi*. Cf. Part II, notes 37 and 58, supra.

[76]The Latin text uses letters for this series, a use which is inconsistent with the convention used throughout the rest of the commentary. See note 39, supra.

[77]1 Peter 2:18.

[78]Romans 13:1.

[79]Romans 13:7.

[80]Romans 13:5.

[81]Romans 13:1.

[82]The text has *ordinattone*, but should read *ordinatione*.

201

{1052} is established by divine ordinance.[82] "Therefore, he who resists authority has opposed the ordinance of God."[83] But he who opposes the ordinance of God receives condemnation upon himself.[84]

4. Likewise, to be subject to a man is not a fault or an evil, but to the contrary is meritorious. Therefore, it appears that one is not absolved from that servitude through baptism. Thus, just as non-Christians are servants of others, even if they become Christians they are required to be subject.

5. Likewise, on this question there are many authorities which can be obtained like those from all the epistles of St. Paul[85] in which he admonishes servants to be subject to their masters.

But to the contrary, a.[86] The Lord asked of Peter, "From whom do the kings of the earth collect customs or polltax, from their sons or from strangers?"[87] And thereafter: "Consequently the sons are exempt."[88] And the Glossa says: "The sons of the kingdom are exempt in every realm, so much more exempt are the children of that kingdom under which all kingdoms are, in whatever earthly realm."[89] Therefore, if good Christians are sons of [the divine] kingdom, it

---

[83]Romans 13:2.

[84]This sentence is a paraphrase of the second clause of Romans 13:2, as follows: "And they who have opposed will receive condemnation upon themselves.

[85]See Ephesians 6:5; Colossians 3:22; Titus 2:9.

[86]The Latin text uses numbers, rather than letters, for this series, a use which is inconsistent with the convention throughout the rest of the commentary. Cf. notes 39, 44 and 76, supra.

[87]The original gives the citation Matthew 17:24, but the citation should read Matthew 17:25.

[88]The original gives the citation Matthew 17:25, but it should read Matthew 17:26. The full quotation is: "And upon [Peter] saying, 'From strangers,' Jesus said to him, 'Consequently the sons are exempt.'"

[89]Glossa Ordin., in h. l.

appears that they may be restricted to the power of no earthly king. Therefore, they are not required to subject themselves to him in any tribute.

b. Likewise, "But one who looks intently at the perfect law,"[90] and the <u>Glossa</u> explains that "The perfect law of freedom is the law of the Gospel."[91] Therefore, if perfect freedom liberates from every servitude, it appears that everyone who adheres to the law of the Gospel is absolved from every servitude of earthly king.

c. Likewise, charity makes all members of Christ one and makes all things common. Hence, it is said, "All things are yours, whether death or life," and so forth.[92] It makes all one, as the Apostle says,[93] "We are all one in Christ, nor is there a distinction between slave and freeman." Therefore, if charity reduces all members to equality and community, it appears therefore that in possessing charity there is no obligation of servitude.

d. Likewise, the bond of divine law is greater than that of human constitution. Yet the law of the Gospel dissolves the burden of legal servitude which indeed was brought forth from God by Moses. Therefore, it dissolves even more forcefully the burden of human servitude and civil law.

e. Likewise, Anselm says, "Through himself he wanted to redeem, so that he might bring man to the original freedom, and that man might be subject to him, not to man."[94] If therefore we are "bought with a

---

[90] James 1:25. The full quotation reads: "But one who looks intently at the perfect law, the law of liberty, and abides by it, not having become a forgetful hearer but an effectual doer, this man shall be blessed in what he does."

[91] <u>Glossa Ordin</u>., in h. 1.

[92] 1 Corinthians 3:22.

[93] This quotation is actually a paraphrase of Ephesians 2:14 and Colossians 3:11.

[94] <u>Cur Deus Homo</u> 1:5.

price,"[95] namely, "with the blood of a lamb unblemished and spotless,"[96] it appears that we are servants of him alone. Therefore, it does not appear that a Christian man, who is reborn in Christ, is bound to any servitude of an earthly empire.

Response. I respond by saying that, if servitude is opposed to freedom, insofar as freedom is said to be three-fold, namely, freedom from external force, from fault, and from misery, then servitude can be said to be three-fold, which is observed in the restriction of freedom. For with respect to the restriction of freedom from fault, the servitude of sin is observed, of which it is said, "Everyone who commits sin is the slave of sin,"[97] and, "do not let sin reign in your immortal body."[98] With respect to the freedom from misery, the servitude of punishment and death is observed, of which it is said, "Christ being raised from the dead, is never to die again, death is no longer master over him."[99] Yet with respect to the restriction of freedom from external force, the servitude of condition is observed, of which it is said, {1053} "Were you called a slave? Do not worry about it. But if you are able to become free, rather do that."[100] However, this servitude is observed in the constriction of freedom by force, not so far as the internal movement of the will is concerned, which cannot be forced, but so far as concerns the external. And hence servitude was introduced in that one conquered another and he surrendered his servitude. . . .

Since there are three kinds of servitude, one kind has its origins in the others. For the servitude of punishment could not exist unless the servitude of

---

[95] 1 Corinthians 6:20.

[96] 1 Peter 1:19.

[97] John 8:34.

[98] Romans 6:12.

[99] Romans 6:9.

[100] 1 Corinthians 7:21.

fault were to precede it. Nor could the servitude of condition follow unless those both preceded. When therefore someone is reborn in Christ and a Christian is produced, he is freed from the servitude of sin, but still he is not thereby liberated. Rather, he still has the possibility, facility and propensity to return to the same kind of servitude. And hence it is that because of his advancement and humiliation the Lord relinquishes for the same the servitude of death and condition. Hence, Christians and others die, and because of the propensity toward evil and the desires contending in the members, from which wars and quarrels arise, they and other peoples are in need of a leader for an earthly king. And thus, there are among Christians kings and princes, lords and servants, not only in accordance with a human institution, but also with a divine dispensation. And in accordance with the distinction of power, they are subject and required as more and less. And this the Lord himself says: "Render to Caesar the things that are Caesar's, and to God the things that are God's."[101] And the Apostle teaches this and condemns those making contrary pronouncements. For he says: "Let all who are under the yoke as slaves regard their own masters as worthy of all honor so that the name of God and our doctrine may not be spoken against. If anyone advocates a different doctrine and does not agree with sound words, those of our Lord Jesus Christ, he is conceited and understands nothing,"[102] and so forth. He proves this in Romans 13:1, and he teaches this in many other passsages, and commends it. Thus it is conceded that Christians are obligated to earthly lords, but not in all things, only in those which are not contrary to God. Not all things, but in those which are rationally established in accordance with right custom, such as tribute, taxes and things similar in all respects. Hence the authorities and reasons which prove this are to be conceded.

1. Therefore, as to what is first objected, concerning the text of Matthew and its gloss, I respond by saying that the text is to be understood as of Christ, that Christ was not required to render tribute, and of those who are his perfect imitators, namely, the Apostles for that they were naturally free and were discharged of all temporal goods. And thus the kings

---

[101] Matthew 22:21.

[102] 1 Timothy 6:1, 3-4.

of the earth were not obliged to receive census or tribute from them. However, that authority is not to be understood as referring to other Christians, either those who are of a servile condition or those who abound in temporal goods.

2. As to what is objected, to the effect that the law of the Gospel is the law of perfect freedom, I respond by saying that it is said to be the law of perfect freedom because it frees us from the servitude of transgression, or even from the servitude of Law, since the spirit of charity, which is the spirit of freedom, is given by what the Apostle says:[103] "For you have not received a spirit of slavery leading to fear again, but you have received a spirit of adoption as sons." And thus from this it does not follow that man, who is under the law of the Gospel, is freed from the servitude of an earthly power.

3. As to what is objected, to the effect that charity unites all, and makes all common, I respond by saying that this {1054} is true by a certain participation, but it is not true of the authority of civil power.[104]

4. As to what is objected, to the effect that the law of the Gospel absolves us from the burden of the Mosaic law, and thus even more so from human law, I respond by saying that it is not the same thing, because that law completes and voids the other law, just as truth does figure. However, it is not this way with the law of human institutions, which supports the observation of the divine law. And hence the Apostle urges prayers for the princes "in order that we may lead a quiet and tranquil life" under them.[105]

5. As to what is objected, to the effect that Christ wanted to redeem us through himself, so that he might bring man to original freedom, I respond by saying that there the full effect of the redemption effected through Christ is noted. But still, we do not fully gain that effect in the present, until "creation will be set free from its slavery to corruption into

---

[103] Romans 8:15

[104] Per auctoritatem dominii.

[105] 1 Timothy 2:2.

the freeedom of the glory of the children of God."[106] Hence, here freedom from guilt is begun, but there freedom from misery and from every human power is consummated. Hence, it does not follow that, if we are ransomed by Christ, because of this we are no longer servants of another, because the dominion of Christ permits the dominion of man, at most in the things which command nothing against God. But it does not permit dominion of the devil or sin, as is said: "No one can serve two masters."[107] Thus, although we are released by the redemption of Christ from the servitude of mortal sin, nevertheless we are not released from the servitude of condition or death.

Question II[108]

Whether the religious are required to obey their prelates in all things which are not contrary to God.
Accordingly, it is asked whether the religious are required to obey their prelates in all things which are not contrary to God. And it appears that:

1. First, by the authority of the Lord: "The scribes and the Pharisees have seated themselves in the chair of Moses; therefore all that they tell you, do."[109] Therefore, if the Lord urges without distinction that what they say is to be done, even of evil prelates, it appears that they are to be obeyed in all things. If you say that this is not to be understood except as to those things which they say and to which man is bound by the mandate of the law, this is contrary, because the Lord says elsewhere: "The one who listens to you listens to me, and the one who rejects you rejects me."[110] Therefore, if God is to be listened to in all things and rejected in nothing, it

---

[106]Romans 8:21.

[107]Matthew 6:24.

[108]The statement of the question here significantly narrows the scope of the inquiry, as compared with Bonaventure's original formulation in the introductory paragraphs of Article III. Cf. text at note 75, supra.

[109]Matthew 23:2-3.

[110]Luke 10:16.

appears that the prelates established by God ought to be obeyed by their subjects in all things.

2. Likewise, "Children, be obedient to your parents in all things."[111] Therefore, if physical children ought to obey physical parents in all things, and spiritual children ought not to obey spiritual fathers less than physical ones do the physical, then the religious ought to obey their prelates in all things.

3. Likewise, blessed Benedict says in his Rules, "If the prelate orders the impossible, it should be done."[112] Therefore, if he is to be obeyed in impossible things, much more so in possible things, and therefore in all.

4. Likewise, Hieronymous says, "You should fear the prefect of the monastery as a lord, esteem him highly as a father. You should believe whatever he will have said to worship, and not judge the opinion of greater men {1055} of whom it is a duty to obey and fulfill their orders, Moses having said, 'Hear, Israel, and do.'"[113]

5. Likewise, Hugh of St. Victor says, "Obedience is a virtue which encompasses all things enjoined to be fulfilled as necessary, unless the authority of the ordinary will oppose."[114] Therefore, it appears that, if the religious does not obey in all things, he doers not possess true obedience. Therefore, if he is required to possess true obedience, he is required to obey in all things.

6. Likewise, it appears to be the case by reason. Just as a man vows poverty and continence, so also does he vow obedience. But he who vows continence is required to abstain from sexual intercourse altogether, and he who vows poverty is required to renounce all temporal goods. Therefore, he who vows obedience is required to obey in all things which are enjoined upon

---

[111] Colossians 3:20.

[112] *Regulae*, ch. 68.

[113] *Ad Rusticum*, Epistle 125, n. 15. Hieronymous paraphrases Deuteronomy 27:9.

[114] *De stat. virtut.*, p. 2, n. 20.

him. Therefore, . . . one should be judged disobedient if he transgresses even one word of the prelate. Therefore, he is required to obey the prelate in all things.

But to the contrary, a. "We must obey God rather than men."[115] Therefore, we are required to obey God in certain things in which we are not required to obey men. Therefore, it appears that we are not required to obey a prelate in all things.

b. Likewise, Bernard says, "The subject is to be inhibited neither without regard to what is promised, nor beyond what is ordered by the law of obedience."[116] Therefore, if any prelate orders him beyond what he promised, it does not appear that he is required to obey him.

c. Likewise, the perfection of religion at most consists in the perfection of obedience. Therefore, if all religious were required to obey in all things, all religious would be equal in perfection. Yet this is plainly false, therefore, and so forth.

d. Likewise, the religious is not required to obey his prelate except by the law of the vow. But by the law of the vow, man is not required to be exempted except that which he vows spontaneously. Therefore, it appears that the prelate cannot exact from him except what he promised to observe.

Response. I respond by saying that one thing is to be said concerning the obedience to be shown a prelate by a religious subject, as to the perfection of obedience, another as to the obligation of necessity. If we speak of it as to perfection, then it is to be said, as Bernard says, "Perfect obedience is ignorant of its end,"[117] and perfect obedience not only in the things which he urges, but even beyond those things. It has this apparent condition for the subject of the precept of the prelate, who desires to imitate him who, humiliating himself, "is made obedient to the father,

---

[115]Acts 5:29.

[116]De dispensatione et praecepto 5:11.

[117]Ibid. 6:12.

even to the point of death."[118] However, if we speak of obedience as to necessary obligation, then it possesses a limit and a measure, according to the magnitude of the vow made. For they are not required to obey their prelates more, except in those things "which they promised the Lord to observe and which are not contrary to the spirit and their rules."[119] Hence, if the prelate ordered anything that was beyond the vow, the subject is not required to comply. And so it is to be conceded that the religious are not required to obey their prelates in all things, although it is safe counsel that they obey in all things that are not contrary to God. Hence, the reasons which were introduced in the second part are to be conceded, since they draw a true conclusion.

1. Therefore, as to what is first objected to the contrary, {1056} that we are to be obedient in all things to those who are in cathedra, this is true of those things for which they look to the chair of authority and the precepts of the law. However, as to other things, it is not mandated. As to what is objected, to the effect that the Lord himself says, "The one who listens to you," and so forth, I respond by saying that it is true that he speaks of these things which the Apostles and their successors mandate from the person of Christ and also from the authority given to them. Still, in nothing that they say is their authority to be rejected. Hence, although we are not held to obey the prelates in all things, still we are required not to reject any mandates of theirs. Hence, it is said in canon law that "the opinion of the pastor, whether just or unjust, is to be feared."

2. As to what is objected, concerning the expression of the Apostle, "Children be obedient to your parents in all things," it is to be said that, if it is understood as being of these things which look to a divine mandate, it is a precept. However, concerning other things, it is an admonition, not a precept.

3-5. As to that expression of blessed Benedict, and Hieronymous and Hugh, it is to be said that they

---

[118] Philippians 2:8.

[119] The reference is to the Regula Fratrum Minorum, ch. 10.

were not speaking of obedience as to the obligation of necessity, but as to the perfection of charity.

6. As to what is objected, to the effect that, just as man vows poverty and continence, so also he vows obedience, I respond by saying that it is both so and not so. It is indeed so in what dominion removes to itself of its own will. However, it is not so because the man does not bind himself to do all that may be commanded of him, but only those things which are expressed in the <u>Regula</u>. And since in every perfect religious order the renunciation is limited essentially so far as to carnal activity and so far as to proprietary activity, either in particular or in general, nevertheless not all things which can be ordered are thus ordered. Therefore, he is not bound to obey in all things. . . . However, the reason for this is that it is possible for someone to renounce property, and even easily enough, especially where possession is had in common. But to comply with all things that are said, here not only is it not easy, it is impossible. And so limits are set to the promise of obedience. They are not thus set for the promise of poverty or even chastity. Hence in the <u>Regula</u> of Francis it is ordered absolutely that those professing those rules may possess nothing at all upon earth. Also, it is ordered absolutely not only to refrain always from the sexual act, but also to abstain from suspect association with and counsel of women. But it is not absolutely commanded of brothers that they obey their prelates in all things, but "in all things which they have promised the Lord to obey and which are not contrary to the spirit and their rules." I do not know if anybody knows anything more to add to any of those vows. Accordingly, in this height of perfection it is fitting to end the discourse on the aforementioned question.

Doubts concerning the Writings of the Master

Doubt I

In this part of the commentary questions concerning the text are presented. And first there is a question concerning the following response which the Master makes: "But it is known that the Apostle was speaking of secular authority."[120] For it does not ap-

---

[120] See Part I, text at note 17, supra.

pear that the Master sufficiently resolved the question presented. To the contrary, he avoids it, since, as we know from the preceding chapter, the devil does not possess the power to do evil from himself, but from God. When, therefore, the Apostle says that "All power is from God,"[121] he understood not only the power of man, but {1057} also that of the devil. Likewise, it appears that his power is not to be resisted, because in the passage, "The people and the kingdom that will not serve him, Nebuchadnezzar," and so forth,[122] the Lord threatens those who would not serve Nebuchadnezzar. Therefore, if by Nebuchadnezzar the devil is signified, it appears, and so forth. Likewise, we ought not resist the power of the devil's agents, namely, evil prelates and tyrants who are agents of the devil. Therefore, much more so is it the case that we ought not resist the devil himself, who is the head of these evil ones.

Response

I respond by saying that the Master correctly says that the passage from the Apostle, that the power is not to be resisted, is to be understood as concerning human authority, not diabolic authority, since human authority is both ordained and frequently moves and commands in an orderly manner. And so "he who resists it has opposed the ordinance of God,"[123] at least if it commands in an orderly manner. But since the devil, from the perversity of his will, always moves toward evil and away from God, then according to the correct order of things and the mandate of the Apostle,[124] we are most particularly to resist him and struggle against him, as against the worst adversary. Therefore,

---

[121]Romans 13:1.

[122]Jeremiah 27:8. The full text of this passage reads as follows: "'And it will be that the nation or kingdom which will not serve him, Nebuchadnezzar king of Babylon, and which will not put its neck under the yoke of the king of Babylon, I will punish that nation with the sword, with famine, and with pestilence,' declares the Lord, 'until I have destroyed it by his hand.'"

[123]Romans 13:2.

[124]The allusion may be to 1 Peter 5:8.

as to what was said to the effect that the power of the devil is from God, I respond by saying that it is true. But he does not use it for the purpose that God gave it to him. On the contrary, he directs his thoughts always toward evil. And when we resist him strongly, we convert his evil into our good.

As to what is objected concerning the agents of the devil, I respond by saying that it is not the same. For his agents do not always move toward evil as he who is inflexible in evil and from whom all evil took its origin.

Doubt II

Likewise, a question arises concerning the following passage: "Direct your attention to the degrees of authority in human affairs. If what the procurator commands," and so forth.[125] In this passage he intimates that, if an inferior authority opposes a superior one, the latter rather than the former is to be obeyed. But to the contrary, "And to the angel of the Church in Pergamum write: 'The archbishop will not dare to set his hand over the subjects of the bishop without him.'"[126] But here the bishop can act without the archbishop. Therefore, it seems that the inferior is to be obeyed rather than the superior. Likewise, a direct authority exercises greater influence than an indirect one. Thus, if the inferior authority is more direct than the superior, then it appears that the inferior authority is to be upheld over the superior. To the contrary of this Boethius says that whatever the inferior power can do, the superior can do, but not conversely.[127] Therefore, the superior power can restrain the inferior. Therefore, its mandate is upheld.

Response

I respond by saying that one can speak in two ways concerning superior and inferior authority. First, the inferior power may flow totally from the superior for which it was ordained, as the authority of the commmis-

---

[125]See Part I, text at note 19, supra.

[126]Apocalypse 2:12.

[127]The reference is apparently to De consolatione philosophiae 5:4.

sioner does from the authority of the proconsul, and that of the proconsul from that of the emperor. And then it is true that the authority of the superior is to be upheld over that of the inferior. Or, second, those authorities may both flow from a superior, and in specific cases the one is placed over the other, and that third authority has power over both, as the authority of the bishop and the archbishop from the pope, who has full power over both. And then it is not generally true that one ought to obey the superior authority rather than the inferior, namely the authority of the archbishop rather than the bishop, since one is a direct prelate, the other indirect. But as to him who possesses {1058} full authority over both, it is true, since he is not merely an indirect prelate. Hence, the subject ought to conform to the mandate of the pope rather than any inferior prelate. And Augustine speaks to this case. And by this the response to the objections is clear.

Doubt III

Finally, a question is raised concerning those authorities the Master cites in the text. For if the question concerns the power for sin,[128] it appears that he is less correct in citing those authorities which speak of the power for ruling and causing the evil which consists of punishment, as observation makes clear.

And I respond by saying that, in consequence, by another mode they can be applied to the case in question. However, as is clearly evident, the Master brings them forward somewhat less accurately. Still, it is not to be wondered at if in so many and such fine writings the Master said something that was less than complete. Nor is he to be insulted on this account. For by his labor he has earned study and gratitude rather than reproofs. It is allowed that in certain passages he may have departed from common opinion and may have adhered to the less probable side, particularly in eight places. . . .[129]

---

[128] *Potestate peccandi*.

[129] There follows at this point in the original text a short discussion by Bonaventure of eight passages, dealing with theological issues unrelated to the philosophical problem discussed in Distinction 44, in

On these eight assertions, the Parisian doctors in general do not follow the Master. Nor do I believe that he is to be sustained in all of these, lest prejudice be done to truth out of love for the man. And all of these things have been clearly shown by his passages and will be manifest.

However, if for any of these it appears to otherwise, and perhaps better, I do not show envy. But I do ask that, if anyone were to find anything in my explanation in this little work of the two preceding books, or of the two which follow, worthy of approval, he may express thanks to God, a liberal giver of goods. In other places where he may have found anything false, doubtful or obscure, he may benevolently give pardon for this insufficent writing, which without doubt, by the witness of conscience, longed very much to speak what was true, clear and universally accepted. . . .

~~~

---

which Bonaventure believes Lombard may have erred.

INDEX

A

Abelard 3.

Albert 10, 86.

Alexander IV, Pope 13.

Alexander of Hales 5, 25, 105.

angels, orders of (in Aquinas' Commentary) 153.

Anselm 51, 129.

anthropology, philosophical 14, 17.

Aquinas xi, xii, xiv, xv, 3, 5-19, 21, 23-25, 27-30, 32, 40-50, 51, 53-58, 60-63, 66, 69-76, 78-83, 86, 87, 89-109, 111, 113, 114, 116, 118-133.

Aristotelianism 6, 9, 11, 23, 28, 82, 112.

Aristotle xiv, xv, 9, 10, 11, 15, 17, 24, 28, 29, 39, 53, 60-64, 76, 81, 82, 85, 86, 89, 92, 108-110, 112, 124.

articulus (or article) 47, 75, 81, 106, 109.

auctoritas 47, 54, 57, 59, 61, 64, 80, 92.

Augustine xiv, 7, 9, 19, 24, 33, 36, 54, 60, 63, 76, 82, 92, 105, 109, 112, 123, 124, 131.

Augustinianism 6, 9.

authority, civil, resistance to see resistance to authority.

B

baccalaureus biblicus xii.

baccalaureus sententiarus 5-7.

Bonaventure xi, 4, 11-13, 25, 29, 30, 32, 40, 42-45, 74, 104-123, 125-133.

C

Caesar 67, 68, 71.

Carlyle, R.W. & A.J. xiv, 15-18, 39, 73, 78.

Catejan 8.

Chenu, M.-D. xii, xiii, 4-7, 10-12, 46, 47, 85, 86.

Christians, duty of obedience of (in Aquinas' Commentary) 161-164. (in Bonaventure's Commentary) 201-207.

Cicero 67, 68, 71.

Commentary on the Meta

physics of Aristotle (Aquinas) 92.

Commentary on the Nicomachean Ethics (Aquinas) 85, 89.

Commentary on the Politics (Aquinas) 85, 92.

Commentary on the Sentences, Aquinas (see also sentential commentary) (translation) 141-173.

Commentary on the Sentences, Bonaventure (see also sentential commentary) (translation) 175-215.

convention(al) (view of civil authority as) xiv, xv, 15, 19, 20, 39, 41, 59, 60, 61, 68, 73, 81-82, 87, 94-96, 124, 132, 133.

Cur Deus Homo (of Anselm 129.

D

Dante 78.

De Civitate Dei 19, 60, 92, 123, 124.

De Benedictis, Matthew M. 105, 133.

de la Rochelle, Jean see Rochelle, Jean de la.

De officiis (of Cicero) 67.

De regimine Judaeorum (of Aquinas) 84, 95.

De regimine principum (of Aquinas) 24, 79, 84, 86, 88, 95, 97, 100, 101.

Degnan, Daniel A. 87.

d'Entreves, A. P. xii, xv, 3, 12-14, 20, 21, 38, 39, 69, 83-87, 89.

Distinction 44 (Sentences) xi, 23-27, 29-31, 37, 42, 45.

divisio textus 46, 48-49, 106, 143.

dominium 143.

Dunbabin, Jean 9, 29, 101.

E

expositio (textus) 7, 48.

emperor, struggle between pope and 15, 16.

F

Fairweather, Eugene R. 10, 11.

Finnis, John 87.

G

Gilson, Etienne 8, 11-15, 74, 78, 104, 105, 106, 112.

H

Henle, R.J. 80.

Henry, Desmond Paul 4, 80.

Henry of Brabant 10.

I

In Libros Politicorum (Aquinas) see Commentary on the Politics.

innocence, state of (in Aquinas' Commentary) 152-155. (in Bonaventure's Commentary) cf. 195-200.

Institutes (of Justinian) 118, 124.

Isidore 16.

J

Jarrett, Bede 132.

John of Salisbury 16.

Jones, W.T. 68, 130.

Justinian 118.

L

lectio 4-7.

Lombard, Peter (see also Sentences) xi, xii, 3-7, 20, 24, 25, 27, 29-37, 39-44, 47-50, 55, 75, 76, 80, 83, 106, 107, 112, 130, 131.

M

magister xi, 4, 5, 105.

Maurer, Armand A. 8.

Moerbeke (Moerbecke) see William of Moerbeke.

Metaphysics (of Aristotle) 28, 52, 54.

Mondin, B. xiii, 46, 81.

Morrall, John B. xv, 3, 4, 10, 14, 15, 17, 18, 24, 29, 34, 68, 96.

Mullane, D. T. 11-13, 28.

N

natural (view of civil authority as) xv, 16, 18-20, 59, 87, 96, 132.

Neoplatonism 9.

Nicomachean Ethics (of Aristotle) 60, 62, 64, 65, 76, 85, 86.

nisi forte 79, 80, 104, 173.

O

obedience, nature of (see also Christians, duty of obedience of) (in Aquinas' Commentary) 156-161.

P

patristic view of civil authority 16, 21.

Peter of Poitiers 4.

political animal (see also, "political animal, social and," "social animal") xv, 15, 87, 88, 90, ("animal civile," "animal sociale") 89.

political animal, social and (see also "political animal," "social animal") 88, 90, 94, ("animal sociale et politicum") 89.

Politics (of Aristotle) xiv, 17, 62, 85, 86, 88, 92.

pope & emperor, struggle between 15, 16.

potentia 143.

potential (or power) for sin (in Sentences) 137-139. (in Aquinas' Commentary) 145-148. (in Bonaventure's Commentary) 179-184.

potential for sin as evil (in Bonaventure's Commentary) 184-189.

potestas 143.

power 143.

praelatio 143.

Q

quaestio (or question) 46, 50, 81, 106.

R

Regula 75.

religious, duty of obedience of (in Aquinas' Commentary) 165-168. (in Bonaventure's Commentary) 207-211.

resistance to authority (in Sentences) 139-140. (in Aquinas' Commentary) 161-164. (in Bonaventure's Commentary) 201-207.

respondeo (dicendum) 47, 106, 107.

rex 17, 24, 73, 77, 131, 173.

Rochelle, Jean de la 105.

Rousseau 18.

rulers, absolute (in Aquinas' Commentary) 161-164.

S

sacerdos 17, 24, 73, 77, 131, 173.

Scotus, Duns 25.

sed contra 47, 48, 52, 53, 56, 57, 61, 75, 106, 107.

Sentences xi, 3, 4, 6-8, 11, 24-27, 30, 45, 83. (translation) 135-140.

sentential commentary (see also Commentary on the Sentences, Aquinas; Commentary on the Sentences, Bonaventure) xi, xii, xiii, xiv, 7, 8, 11, 42, 45, 46, 80, 81.

Simon, Yves 21, 91-92.

social animal (see also "political animal," "political animal, social and") 88, 90.

solutio 47, 48, 53, 57, 59, 75, 107.

sovereignty, source of (in Aquinas' Commentary) 149-151. (in Bonaventure's Commentary) 190-200.

Summa Contra Gentiles (of Aquinas) 87, 91, 94, 100.

Summa Theologiae (of Aquinas) xiii, 8, 23, 46, 63, 64, 79, 86-89, 91, 95-98, 100, 103.

Synan, Edward S. 6, 131.

T

textus 8.

Topics (of Aristotle) 110.

tractatio quaestionum 106.

tyrants see rulers, absolute.

U

Urban IV, Pope 10, 13.

Ullmann, Walter xv, 9, 10, 16, 18, 19, 34, 90, 117.

V

Vio, Cardinal Thomas de 8.

W

William of Moerbeke 10, 11, 89.

Wolter, Allan B. 106.

About the Author

MICHAEL P. MALLOY received his B.A. and Ph.D. from Georgetown University and his J.D. from the University of Pennsylvania. He is currently Associate Professor of Law at Seton Hall University. He previously taught at New York Law School and has lectured at Thessaloniki University in Greece, under the auspices of the Institute of International Public Law and International Relations. Prior to entering law teaching, he served as Special Counsel with the U.S. Securities and Exchange Commission, and as Attorney-Adviser with the Office of the Comptroller of the Currency and with the U.S. Treasury Department's Office of Foreign Assets Control. He was the recipient of the Treasury Department's Special Achievement Award, in recognition of his efforts during the Iran hostage crisis from 1979 through 1980. He is the author of numerous articles, reports and comments in the fields of international law, banking law and political philosophy. He is a member of Phi Beta Kappa, the American Society of International Law and the Hegel Society of America, among other professional and scholarly organizations.